Battlegrc
BOLSI

2010

011

Battleground Europe

BOESINGHE

Stephen McGreal

Series editor
Nigel Cave

Pen & Sword
MILITARY

First published in Great Britain in 2010 by
PEN AND SWORD MILITARY
an imprint of
Pen & Sword Books Ltd
47 Church Street
Barnsley
South Yorkshire
S70 2AS

ISBN 9781848840461

Typeset in Times

Printed and bound in England by
CPI UK

Pen & Sword Books Ltd incorporates the imprints of Pen & Sword Aviation, Pen &
Sword Maritime, Pen & Sword Military, Wharncliffe Local History, Pen & Sword Select,
Pen & Sword Military Classics and Leo Cooper.

For a complete list of Pen & Sword titles please contact
PEN & SWORD BOOKS LIMITED
47 Church Street, Barnsley, South Yorkshire, S70 2AS, England
E-mail: enquiries@pen-and-sword.co.uk
Website: www.pen-and-sword.co.uk

CONTENTS

SERIES EDITOR

Boesinghe is not a place name that often comes up in battlefield touring; in fact the northern tip of the Salient is notable for the relative paucity of its visitors, in the past with the sole exception of Essex Farm Cemetery and, nowadays, some more adventurous souls who manage to find their way to 'Yorkshire Trench'. Some years ago the east side of the canal was relatively undeveloped; but the last decade and more has witnessed the development of a significant sized industrial park that has seemed to envelop some of the small, isolated cemeteries that were a characteristic of much of the ground covered in this book. To be frank, it has never been an area of scenic beauty: flat (though small rises in the ground had a tremendous importance during trench holding operations) and uninspiring seems to sum it up.

Yet during the months and years between late October 1914 and September 1918 large numbers of units spent periods of time of dreary discomfort in water and mud, interspersed with tragedy, death and maiming, in this northernmost outpost of the Salient. Significant events happened – the fighting at Second Ypres in 1915 and the push forward on 31st July 1917 (what an optimistic day that was; and what a false dawn it proved to be!); but the memory of the area was generally one of trench warfare, arguably an example of it at its grimmest.

This book gives a flavour of these months of trench warfare: short entries in war diaries, filled with routine and interspersed with trench raids, small and large, as both sides sought local advantage. The big occasions also have their place. The extensive tours section takes the visitor around the battlefield and provides points where it is possible to gain an appreciation of the issues that faced the rival armies. The canal zone itself is well covered and advantage is taken of the public walkway along the canal bank near Essex Farm to explain those mouldering bunkers dug into the canal embankments that could be spotted as a battlefield visitor sped north to better known places, such as the Trench of Death at Dixmuide or out to the east of the Salient, to Langemark and beyond.

Boesinghe is a book that helps to fill the gaps left in the series' coverage of the Salient. So, at last, men who fought here, who were wounded and maimed and died here, have a book to themselves which will help us to understand what they did and achieved; and to be able to go to where they did it.

Nigel Cave,
Collegio Rosmini, Stresa: January 2010.

INTRODUCTION

FORGOTTEN BATTLEFIELD REDISCOVERED headlined the media, as television crews beamed images of an excavated First World War trench system and the gruesome discovery of skeletal human remains. For a brief few days in the late nineties, the Boesinghe trench system, dormant and forgotten for some eighty years, again became news-worthy even featuring in a special BBC edition of 'Meet the Ancestors'. The discovery came about due to the impending redevelopment of formerly undisturbed agricultural fields into an industrial complex. The credit for the discovery goes to an enthusiastic group of Belgians known as the 'Diggers', who under a special license from the Flemish Regional authorities excavated the site while keeping one step ahead of the advances of huge earth moving plant. The 'Diggers' unearthed a trench system and communication centre that provided an invaluable insight into trench warfare and trench construction in a water logged, persistently shelled, British sector.

Sadly, in the name of progress, the majority of the site has disappeared beneath the industrial units, but a sanitised modern representation, tracing a section of the original line of 'Yorkshire Trench', is retained for posterity. This modern exhibit, the nearby graves of two legendary Celtic poets and also Essex Farm, where the then Lieutenant John McCrae penned the classic poem, 'In Flanders Fields', act as a magnet for battlefield visitors. The less informed visitor might assume the area was of little military significance, when in reality for two years Boesinghe represented the northern limit of the British front line. The cluster of military cemeteries within the sector is a reminder of the consequences of holding this vital stretch of the line throughout the years of carnage.

The Boesinghe canal sector was the extreme northern limit of the Ypres salient, where parts of the far left of the British front line stood within a long stone's throw of the German positions. The eastern canal bank, facing Boesinghe, became a fiercely contested frontline where continual bombardments ensured St Peter met an unending trickle of defenders from the Boesinghe 'quiet sector', where the lines attracted a disproportionate amount of explosive and gas shelling from the enemy. There were no glorious charges in the immediate area of Boesinghe, nothing for the fortunate survivors to reflect back on in the autumn of their lives, except for the horrors and depravation of a miserable existence in the line.

The Germans briefly occupied Boesinghe; they withdrew to higher ground in early October 1914, leaving Boesinghe in flames. Today we casually stroll along the once heavily shelled canal bank, where vigilant snipers searched for a victim who perhaps dallied a little too long, until the crack of a Mauser rifle abruptly ended another young life. Life and death here was as unpredictable as any area of the Western Front, for holding and maintaining the line with all its inherent dangers and constant patrol work exacted a severe toll on the personnel. One account refers to the canal embankment with its network of dugouts as,

> *A town with all the variety and interest of a densely populated industrial area, which in many respects it greatly resembled. The accommodation was very bad at first – it improved later, affording little comfort or safety to its harassed population. The death rate was heavy, despite the abundance of fresh air, and minor casualties frequent, but there was no birth rate. Its cemeteries were an obvious reminder of the terms and conditions of existence in that neighbourhood.*

Always overshadowed by the destruction of Ypres, the front line at Boesinghe, living up to its tag of 'Forgotten Battlefield', has received minimal coverage. Great War enthusiasts, all too familiar with many infamous names of pulverised rubble where our forebears fought and died, are often unaware of Boesinghe, where the incessant steady toll of casualties of this 'quiet sector' claimed its share of a 'lost generation'. This work is an attempt to address this imbalance and ensure those who fell in this sector are not forgotten. I hope that no longer will my mention of Boesinghe be met with a querulous, 'Where's that?'.

As with my other Battleground book, *Zeebrugge and Ostend Raids*, I am again grateful to Pen and Sword for allowing me the opportunity to publish this concise history.

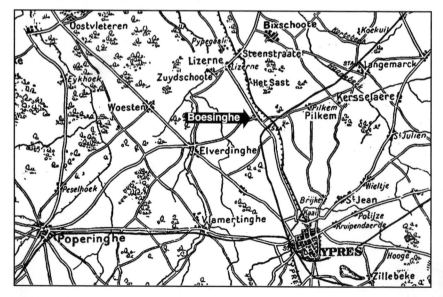

ACKNOWLEDGEMENTS

I would like to thank the following: Nigel Cave who has undertaken a thorough review of this work and patiently corrected copy; however any errors are solely my responsibility. The Commonwealth War Graves Commission enquiry section, particularly Roy Hemington. Alan Gregson deserves a special mention, for he accompanied the author to Boesinghe and studiously juggled a collection of old and new maps, as we navigated our route around the former battlefields. Eirian Griffiths for the image and details of Private E. Jones. The author, noted historian and former Punk Rock band member Peter Hart, who kindly provided archive material. Andrew MacKay for his East Lancashire Regiment material. Anne Pedley and the team at the Regimental Archives of the Royal Welsh Fusiliers for generously providing copies of war diaries and private letters for use in this publication. Dennis Reeves, curator of the Liverpool Scottish archives, for details on casualties. To fellow WFA member Peter Threlfall for searching through his book collection for any references or images connected to Boesinghe. Battleground Series Design Manager and friend Roni Wilkinson for his customary good humour and patience while producing the finished article. This work is enhanced by several atmospheric photographs depicting canal-side defences and a view of Farm 14 provided by him. Friend and fellow author Ted Smith for research material and some images. The staff of the National Archives, Kew. Finally my family, especially my wife Ann, for her tolerance and understanding during my absence from family life as I burnt the midnight oil trying to create a reasonable account from the reams of research material amassed. Without their co-operation Dad's latest project would not have come to fruition. Thank you.

ADVICE FOR VISITORS.

For a tour of the sites within this guide the traveller will find his own vehicle and a decent pair of walking shoes are the most convenient means of touring. In advance of the trip the motorist is advised to consult the continental traffic regulations. Apart from the obvious difference of driving on the right, traffic priorities vary considerably. The French and Belgian speed limits are as vigilantly enforced as in this country but there is one notable difference; speeding motorists are subject to an on the spot fine, payable in the local currency. You must also be able to produce your vehicle documentation and driving licence; both parts of the new style licence are required by law. Satellite navigation systems equipped with a radar speed trap warning device are illegal in France; the police will take draconian measures against a motorist, even if the device is switched off.

The rear of your vehicle must bear a GB sticker; these are often included with your vehicle channel crossing ticket. Headlamp beam adaptors (a self-adhesive plastic lens) are required; otherwise, your vehicle is legally unfit for use; in the event of an accident, this could invalidate your insurance. European Motoring Regulations demand vehicles carry spare exterior bulbs, an advance warning triangle visible at a distance of fifty metres, first aid kit, and a high visibility jacket. Belgian law requires vehicles to carry a fire extinguisher, which must be accessible from the driver's seat. Should you choose to ignore this advice, please bear in mind the small print in your insurance policy, for it is the

The Menin Gate Memorial to the missing.

responsibility of the driver to ensure his vehicle complies with the law and is roadworthy for the country he visits. Failure to comply might invalidate your insurance in the event of an accident.

A recent survey revealed a high percentage of United Kingdom motorists are unaware that their fully comprehensive motoring insurance reduces to Third Party cover when driving abroad. Contact your insurer and advise them of your travel plans and the duration of the visit; for an additional fee, you will receive temporary full cover. Your roadside breakdown policy does not extend to the continent unless you also pay a modest charge for temporary extended cover. The channel tunnel operator also offers the option of an "all in one" motor breakdown and travel insurance. This can be booked online when making your channel crossing arrangements.

When refuelling your vehicle the experience can be a little daunting, given the differences in language and the worrying possibility of filling up with the wrong fuel. The Flemish for unleaded gasoline/petrol is *Loodvril Benzine* and the French equivalent is *Essence sans Plomb*. Diesel is gazole.

Travellers should obtain a free European Health Insurance Card (EHIC), which allows access to most forms of medical and hospital treatment. The EHIC reciprocal medical cover does not cover every thing you might expect from the National Health Service, so take out additional travel insurance. The EHIC forms are available from the Post Office; allow four weeks for the card to arrive. A much faster service is available on www.ehic.uk.com

Under no circumstance should visitors touch any of the assortments of shells and other ordnance that remains on the former battlefields. Such relics are generally corroded to a highly dangerous state, and can still cause severe injury or death. It is reprehensible that some people use metal detectors to locate artefacts on the battlefields, before adding insult to injury by digging for their find. Such deplorable actions on land steeped in our ancestors' blood are not only contrary to the strict laws prohibiting the collection and export of battlefield relics; they desecrate land, which regularly yields the skeletal remains of servicemen. When paying your respects at the Menin Gate memorial, consider where many of the 55,000 who have no known grave lie.

Generally, spring and autumn are the best times to visit the battlefields, as the crops do not disguise the lie of the land and farmers are more disposed to allow access to their fallow fields. Always park away from gateways and keep farm tracks clear; or remain within a few metres of your vehicle if stopping to visit an unexpected memorial or vantage point. In built up areas look for parking regulations signage and also be aware

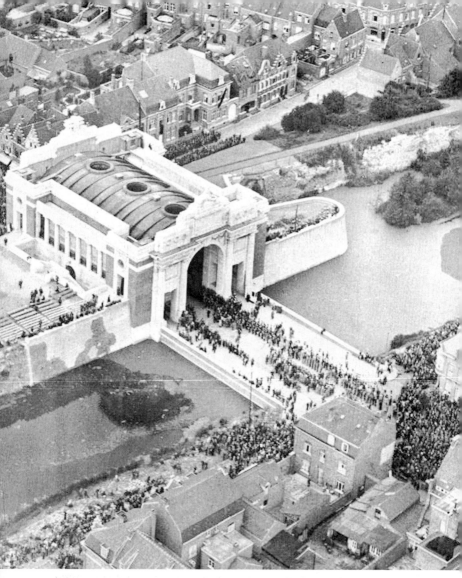

The Menin Gate Memorial's official opening, 1 July 1927.

that a yellow line on the kerb indicates no parking. Most of the woods are private game reserves conserved for hunters; do not enter without permission, especially at weekends, as you may inadvertently be at the receiving end of a shotgun. An unexpected hazard are the Belgium cyclists, who are designated as privileged road users; do not obstruct cycle lanes even momentarily or you will face the ire of the cyclists!

Since the Great War the names of Belgian towns and villages have often altered, as the Flemish version is now used; however they are still

12

recognisable. To avoid any confusion, the names familiar to our forebears appear throughout this work, however it is worth specifically mentioning that Boesinghe is now Boezinghe and Ypres is now Ieper.

From Calais, the motorist should head for the A16 and proceed in the Dunkerque direction towards junction forty-seven. After a couple of miles join the E40 until the N8 turn off. On joining the N8, go to Elverdinghe, at the cross roads turn left, after a short distance turn right for Boesinghe. The journey will take approximately one hour. Should you be staying in Ypres, remain on the N8.

This work provides sufficient information and more than enough maps to navigate your way around the tours; however the traveller may wish to acquire one or two detailed maps covering the wider area. Reprints of French and Belgian sector trench maps are available from G H Smith and Son (www.ghsmith.com/worldwar1) or alternatively telephone +44 (0) 1347 821329. You will require trench map Belgium 28. N.W. 2 edition 6A St. Julien, which shows the trenches, corrected to 30 June 1917. Originally issued at 1:10,000 scale, the modern reprint is seven tenths of the size of the original. Sheet 28 N.W edition 5A Belgium shows Boesinghe in relation to Ypres and includes the rear areas up to Poperinghe. The glossy modern reprint is again seven tenths of the size of the original trench maps and, at 1:20,000 scale, you will find a magnifying glass useful to view trench locations.

The Belgian *Institut Geographique National* or IGN maps are 1:20,000 scale or one centimetre to every 200 metres. These maps are similar to our Ordnance Survey maps; Poperinghe-Ieper 28 1-2 extends as far as the northern fringes of Boesinghe and includes the large towns of Poperinghe and Ieper (Ypres). The IGN maps are available from Hereford Map Centre Ltd (www.themapcentre.com) or telephone +44 (0) 1432 266322. Members of the Western Front Association (WFA) should contact the Commodities Officers, who retail Ypres Map Sheet 28 on a *Mapping the Front* DVD. Another book in the Battleground Europe series slightly overlaps this work; entitled '*Walking the Salient*' by Paul Reed, it is highly recommended. Essentially a walker's guide to the entire Salient, one of the chapters also covers the Boesinghe sector.

The town of Ypres offers a diverse range of accommodation but, due to its popularity, bookings are generally required well in advance of your trip. A good range of accommodation appears on www.greatwar.co.uk; alternatively the following list may be of use. Generally continental star ratings are one below British expectations.

HOTELS

Novotel Ieper Centrum Flanders Fields. A three star hotel, a short stroll from the town centre.

Tel + 32 (0) 57/ 42 96 00. Email h3172@accor.hotels.com

Best Western Flanders Lodge. A four star hotel on the north eastern edge of the town.

Tel + 32 (0) 57/21 70 00. Email bw-ieper@skynet.be

Old Tom. A one star hotel situated on the north side of the main square in Ypres.

Tel. +32 (0) 57/20 15 41. Email info@oldtom.be www.oldtom.be

BED AND BREAKFAST Accommodation

B&B Hortensia. Situated in central Ypres, ten minutes from the Menin Gate.

Tel. + 32 (0) 57/21 24 06. Email info@guesthouse-ypres.be

Ter Thuyne. Situated in central Ypres a few minutes from the market place.

Tel. + 32 (0) 57/36 00 42. Email info@terhuyne.be

Varlet Farm. Farmhouse B&B located nine kilometres from Ypres.

Tel. 0032 (0) 51 777 859. Email info@varletfarm.com
www.varletfarm.com

Bereaved families at Boulogne Station waiting to entrain for the various battlefields.

HOW TO USE THIS BOOK

This modest book aims to provide the reader with an insight into the carnage and self-sacrifice experienced by the troops assigned to the Boesinghe canal sector, north north east of Ypres. Should the contents stir the reader to deep thoughts over the trials and tribulations of the legendary Tommy Atkins, then I have succeeded in my aim.

Before travelling to Belgium relax in your favourite armchair for a few evenings and familiarise yourself with the book's contents, for there is little point arriving at the sites or monuments without having already comprehended their significance. Should you intend visiting a particular grave, remember to take the relevant details obtainable from the Commonwealth War Graves Commission (www.cwgc.org); or by post from their office at 2, Marlow Road, Maidenhead, Berks; or telephone 0171 730 0717. Normally by the entrance to each cemetery a small locker usually contains the cemetery registers, but unfortunately these are sometimes missing. The theft of the cemetery registers prevents visitors

The standard design of CWGC information locker, usually incorporated into a cemetery structure. The smaller cemeteries often do not have these lockers.

from easily finding the precise location of a particular grave within the cemetery; and the almost equally common theft of the visitor book denies the visitor an opportunity to write a comment. An extremely annoying recent development is the defacing of pages bearing the details of an executed soldier. Scrawling 'Shot at Dawn Why' around the name of a man sentenced to death serves no purpose whatsoever in such registers.

The tours at the rear of the book concentrate on the forward areas and, to a lesser extent Elverdinghe, a major billeting and supply area between the canal and Poperinghe. The cobbled thoroughfares of both locations echoed to the steady tramp of army boots as troops marched through them to and from the Salient. The forward areas can be covered by car, foot or bicycle; two leisurely days will be ample to visit every site contained within the guide. There is no need to take any serious hiking or orienteering equipment, just sensible footwear. Before setting off, enjoy a hearty breakfast. Arrange to take a packed lunch and liquid refreshment with you, as this will save disrupting the tour in the quest for sustenance.

In 1906, Rudyard Kipling published *The Widow's Party*, which contained the lines, "A court-house stands where the reg'ment goed and the river's clear where the raw blood flowed". The modern battlefield

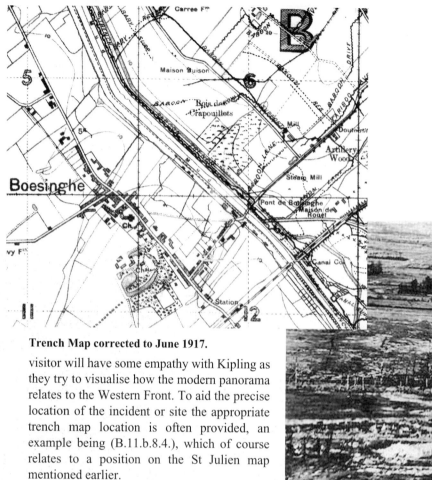

Trench Map corrected to June 1917.

visitor will have some empathy with Kipling as they try to visualise how the modern panorama relates to the Western Front. To aid the precise location of the incident or site the appropriate trench map location is often provided, an example being (B.11.b.8.4.), which of course relates to a position on the St Julien map mentioned earlier.

Period British trench maps are divided into large squares identified by a capital letter (B). These are subdivided into 1,000 yard squares each identified by a number (11) thus B.11 in the above example. The latter squares are divided into four smaller squares equating to 500 yard squares, identified by a lower case a, b, c or d. Square 'a' is the top left hand square, the others in clock wise order are b, d and c, which sits beneath a. Again, our example B.11.b. is now depicting a typical war diary entry for a known sector. The 500-yard squares were also divided into a ten by ten grid of fifty by fifty yard squares. To pinpoint the 8.4 in our example we travel from zero on the extreme left

16

of the square along the X axis (west to east) an imaginary eight squares fifty yards wide, the final reference is four squares up the Y axis (south to north). The trench map location used locates the grounds of Boesinghe Chateau but, given the expanse of the grounds, would require a pinpoint map reference for artillery to locate a precise target. This was achieved by dividing the fifty-yard squares into not a ten by ten matrix but one of a hundred by one hundred.

An aerial view of Boesinghe Chateau and the shattered village.

BOESINGHE

28.B. 11b. 9.5.

Visible on the left are the concrete sandbags of Yorkshire Trench. Some of the pathways replicate the path of other entrenchments.

Over the past two decades Boesinghe has altered considerably, industrial units have encroached on some previously isolated battlefield cemeteries, and there is now a large industrial complex alongside the canal bank, sited on terrain that saw much action during the early years of the war. After much deliberation, the author has included the actions of July 1915, as it seems remiss to publish a Boesinghe guide and exclude them. Furthermore, a tour includes visiting Yorkshire Trench, itself sited within the sprawling industrial park. The guide concentrates on an area of approximately two miles radius from the centre of Boesinghe and progresses towards Pilckem Ridge.

At the front of this book is a listing of *Battleground* titles, several of which deal specifically with the independent actions that collectively constitute the various battles of Ypres. Alternatively, the reader might like to consult one of the scores of books written on these epic Flanders battles.

Chapter One

EARLY DAYS

In 1913, some 18,000 people inhabited Ypres, a thriving centre for the manufacture of lace, woollen goods, and haberdashery; and leather tanneries and dye works provided further employment. The waters of the canalised Yperlee River once ran through the town, permitting boats laden with freight to load or unload directly into the town's warehouses. Prior to 1848, barges still had egress to the western facade of the Cloth Hall. However, by 1914, the canal terminated on the northern fringe of the town, but craft still conveyed goods to and from the Belgian coast twenty-two miles away.

Some 325 yards from the dead end, the waters from the Ypres-Comines canal connected with the *Canal de L'Yser*. This canal ran due north to Dixmuide, roughly parallel with the Ypres-Boesinghe road. The spoil produced during construction of the fifty-yard wide canal formed banks which flanked the canal; tall, bushy topped poplar trees lined both embankments. The canal had a maximum depth of fifteen feet; a narrow single lock at Het Sas maintained the depth and prevented tidal influences extending along the canal. This lock, approximately four miles from Ypres, had a twenty foot rise and fall and incorporated innovative side ponds to recycle a third of the water lost during lock operations; without the lock the water would drain away to the sea.

Near Boesinghe two bridges crossed the *Canal de L'Yser*. The most substantial, situated approximately a half mile south of the village, bore the single track Ypres-Roulers railway; while the *Pont de Boesinghe*

A pre-war view of the dead end, which became known to the troops of the BEF as Tattenham Corner.

Tattenham Corner post war.

swing bridge carried general traffic. The surrounding agricultural fields were dotted with the occasional farmhouse, usually ringed by a moat. The dwellings were unremarkable in every respect, yet the pulverised ruins of some would attain their own unique niche in military history as a place of carnage or a serene war cemetery.

The Flanders fields were no strangers to war, which returned in the autumn of 1914. The Belgium army fought unsuccessfully against the overwhelming might of the invading German army. Three Belgian ports fell prior to 18 October, when a confident German Fourth Army attacked on a frontage extending from the coastal town of Nieuport to Dixmuide, nine miles inland. Another German victory seemed inevitable, however the plucky Belgians made a determined stand on the banks of the River Yser. After ten days of fierce fighting the situation looked so grave that King Albert decided to order the opening of the sluice gates at Nieupoort. The rising waters gradually flooded thousands of hectares of the surrounding polders. Flood water and determined allied counter attacks stemmed the German advance and prevented the turning of the allied flank.

The carefully regulated waist deep inundation forced the enemy to direct blows against the Ypres Salient in an attempt to reach the coast and the 'open' flank. Attacks continued around Nieuport and Dixmuide, and the Yser fighting became merged with the tenacious fighting around Ypres and its satellite villages. The ensuing clash of arms produced by the 'race to the sea' triggered a series of engagements collectively known as the First Battle of Ypres, which officially lasted from 19 October to 22 November 1914. The series of actions are beyond the remit of this work; however, one incident does have a tenuous Boesinghe connection.

The 1/Black Watch (Royal Highlanders) landed at Le Havre on 14 August 1914 as a component of 1 Brigade of the British 1st Division. The professional soldiers were involved in the Retreat from Mons before turning on the enemy at the River Marne, followed by the advance to the Aisne. The division redeployed to the north and, by 21 October, 1/Black Watch were resting near the hamlet of Pilckem, over a mile from Boesinghe. The majority of 1 Brigade deployed in front of the road running between Langemarck and Steenstraat, while dismounted French cavalry held the line on the left of 1/Cameron Highlanders. Centrally between the villages, at the crossroads of the Langemarck to Bixschoote road, stood the café style inn *Kortekeer Cabaret*, now held by a unit of Cameron Highlanders.

The French cavalry lacked entrenching tools and when the enemy attacked early on 22 October the Germans, who now enfiladed the left of 1 Brigade's flank, drove them from their positions. The Camerons were driven from their ditches. Later A, B and C companies of 1/Black Watch, supported by dismounted French cyclists, advanced to restore the situation around the lost *Kortekeer Cabaret*.

Two officers of the battalion were victims of this fighting. Captain Edward F M Urquhart commanded A Company of the 1/Black Watch. He was the thirty-seven year old son of an Edinburgh clergyman and was gazetted to the Black Watch in 1897. He saw action in the South African war and in 1913 held the position of Inspector of Physical Training for the army in Northern India. Also in the unit was Lieutenant Charles

After the innundation.

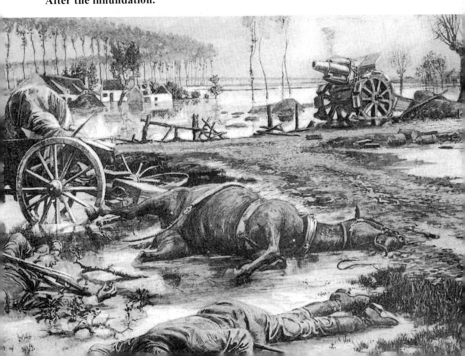

L C Bowes Lyon. He was the eldest son of a former Black Watch lieutenant colonel and cousin to the late Queen Mother. The Lieutenant survived the 29 May 1914 sinking of the *Empress of Ireland*, when 1,000 souls perished.

The Scots set up a machine gun within a ruined windmill a short distance east of the crossroads and inflicted heavy casualties upon the Kaiser's men. All around the fighting intensified and flames consumed the windmill. Major General Bulfin, commanding 2 Brigade, now ordered troops forward and, after severe fighting, by the following nightfall *Kortekeer Cabaret* was again in British possession and the enemy retired. Captain Urquhart and Lieutenant Bowes Lyon are believed to have died repulsing an attack while A Company held a line along the Steenbeek River. The bodies of the fallen officers were not interred on the battlefield but instead

Lieutenant Bowes Lyon.

Men of 12th Battalion, King's Liverpool, in hastily dug rifle pits, prepare to take on German infantry advancing on Ypres.

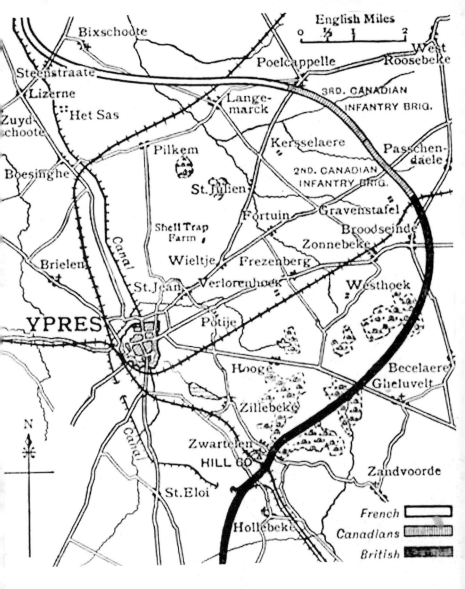

Allied line around Ypres before the gas attack

were carried the mile and a half to Boesinghe churchyard and buried alongside each other. *Soldiers Died in the Great War* lists five other ranks 1/Black Watch casualties for 22 October 1914; they were evidently buried where they fell. Privates J McCormick, R McLellan and E Todd are commemorated on the Menin Gate. After the Armistice, the remains of Lance Corporal S Watters were recovered from the battlefield and re-interred in grave EE 46, Buffs Road Cemetery, north of Wieltje. The

23

CWGC have no details on Private G Boath. Of the thirteen killed the next day, eleven are commemorated on the Menin Gate.

On 24 October French troops relieved the Black Watch, who now headed south to bolster the troops defending the Menin Road. Meanwhile the southern flank received a steady influx of French reinforcements. The attacks faltered, the crisis waned and on 15 November the French assumed responsibility for the seventeen-mile Salient frontage. A week later the curtain came down on the First Battle of Ypres.

German attempts to break through to the channel ports and separate the allied forces failed. The Allies retained Ypres, but the enemy gained further ground along the range of low ridges overlooking the town. From their vantage points, the enemy commenced the systematic shelling of this Flanders town. Mobile warfare had failed to produce a decisive breakthrough, inertia set in and troops consolidated their positions. The pick and shovel became almost as important as the rifle as enemies dug into the earth for cover from the onslaught of shrapnel and bullets; and soon a network of trenches from the North Sea to the Swiss border evolved.

German coastal defences.

Chapter Two

A VERY UNGENTLEMANLY WEAPON

Early in 1915 the first British units returned to the dreaded Salient, initially taking over a five-mile stretch of line in the region of Poelcapelle to the Menin Road. By April, British, Dominion and other Empire troops held two thirds of the Salient. The French 11th Division was gradually relieved by the 1st Canadian Division between 14 and 17 April. Their frontage extended for 4,500 yards in length, arching out to three quarters of a mile forward of the hamlet of Gravenstafel. The Canadians found the defences in a deplorable condition, for the French preferred to maintain a minimal force in the front line. If attacked, the forward troops retired, allowing the French 75 mm artillery to halt the enemy. In the latter years of the conflict the enemy, with great success adapted a modified form of this method of defence in depth. An officer described 2 Brigade's sector as being '*in a deplorable state and in a very filthy condition, all the little broken down side trenches and shell holes apparently being used as latrines and burial places for bodies*'.

As the German bombardments accelerated, the Canadians urgently commenced developing the defences into something akin to British military practice.

The French second line was better prepared for defence than the front line and became known as the GHQ Line. The Official History describes this line in Spring 1915 thus:

> *It ran from Zillebeke Lake, where it was one and a half miles behind the front, northwards to a point half a mile east of Wieltje, where it was three miles behind the front, thence it gradually turned north westwards to join a line covering Boesinghe village and railway bridge. It consisted of well-constructed textbook redoubts, of some thirty yards face, with their flanks turned back, each for a garrison of about fifty men. These redoubts were four or five hundred yards apart and were eventually joined up by fire trenches...*

The first stirrings of spring roused the military machine from its enforced period of winter inactivity. Small-scale hostile activity pre-empted a sustained and determined attempt to capture Ypres. Despite Germany being a signatory to the 1899 Hague Convention prohibiting the 'use of projectiles the object of which is the diffusion of asphyxiating or deleterious gases', the enemy added toxic gases to its arsenal. In October, near Neuve Chapelle, the Germans used shrapnel shells containing irritant gases but to no real avail and a few months later the use of tear gas shells on the Eastern Front also failed. Undeterred, Germany formulated plans for a major release of chlorine vapour. Railheads, already bristling with activity, began to receive thousands of gas cylinders, destined for the Salient. The French were aware of the enemy's intentions due to the 30 March testimony of a prisoner from the German IV Corps.

> There is now a store at the front on the line near Lillebeke containing bombs about 1.40 metres long, placed in casemated shelters. They hold asphyxiating gas. No use has been made of them, but sappers have received instructions as follows. The bombs are to be placed on their sides with their point to the enemy; a wind in the right direction is required. The operators have a peculiar head dress and all the men are to wrap cloth over their nostrils.

Any suspicions of a fanciful account intended to unnerve the Salient's defenders were dispelled following the interrogation of a deserter from the 51st Reserve Division, who surrendered to the French 11th Division prior to its relief by Canadian Forces. The information, released on 15 April, revealed the attack details and the preparations made to release asphyxiating gas. The prisoner spoke of bombs about 80 centimetres high, ranging all along the front of his Corps in the proportion of about twenty of the tubes to each forty metres. [The publication of the deserter's name in a post war article written by the commanding officer of the French 11th Division prompted a German investigation. In 1932, the deserter received a ten-year prison sentence and loss of his civil rights.] The Belgians also captured a prisoner who was carrying a small sack filled with gauze, for dipping in some solution to counter the effect of gas. This gauze was found to contain hyposulphite of soda with one per cent of an unidentifiable substance. He warned of an attack scheduled for 15 April. The date was correct; but unfavourable wind delayed the attack. After three tense days in which the attack failed to materialise, the French dismissed the warnings as a ruse by the enemy to instil fear by the mere threat of the release of such a frightful weapon. However, the Germans were biding their time, waiting for a favourable northeast wind to carry the gas in the direction of the allied army. The slightest exposure to chlorine gas can result in eye irritation or laboured breathing; whilst the inhalation of copious amounts of chlorine damages the lung tissues, incapacitating those exposed to it. In extreme cases, the effect of the gas causes a reaction with the respiratory systems' mucous membranes, filling the lungs with a watery, frothy matter, which gradually increases until it fills the entire respiratory system, causing the death of the victim.

In April 1915 the French relieved the British in the extreme north of the Salient, allowing the British to respond to pressure upon their positions to the south and east. The Belgians continued to hold the flooded sector near Bixschoote, where they stood shoulder to shoulder with the French Eighth Army, led by General Putz. His 87th French Territorial Division and the 45th Algerian Division (colloquially referred to as 'Turcos') held the trenches from Bixschoote on the canal to the Ypres-Poelcapelle road, approximately one mile east of Langemarck. On their right flank stood V Corps, under the command of Lieutenant General Sir Herbert Plumer. In short, two thirds of the Salient were the responsibility of the British Second Army, whilst the French held a five mile front up to Steenstraat, where they linked with the Belgian forces.

In February the 1st Canadian Division arrived in France, became part of Plumer's force and now held 5,000 yards of the line extending from the Ypres-Poelcapelle road along the Gravenstafel Ridge to the Ypres-Roulers railway forward of Zonnebeke, where they linked with the British 27th and 28th Divisions, extending to Hill 60, held by the 5th Division.

The 45th Algerian and 87th Territorial divisions and a small detachment of cavalry made up the *Groupement d' Elverdinghe*, commanded by the GOC 45th Division. On 21 April Colonel Mordacq, the commander of 90 Brigade, 45th Division, spent the day surveying the section of line his men had just taken over, noting:

> *The general terrain is so flat that a slight rise to twenty-five metres, such as at Pilkem, gives it a commanding view. From the ridge, it*

A machine-gun section of Zouaves.

would have been possible for him [Germans] *to see back to Boesinghe and the French and Belgian positions along the canal.*

Across No Man's Land were XXVI Corps, with XV Corps on their right, of Fourth Army, commanded by General Albrecht, Duke of Württemberg.

The wind finally blew from a favourable direction, prompting General von Falkenheyn to order a gas release prior to an infantry attack by the Duke of Württemberg's Fourth Army at 06.45 next day. The German Official History notes: *'Almost throughout the forces, both leaders and troops regarded with mistrust the untried means of offence, if they were not entirely inclined against it'.*

The objective for XXIII Reserve Corps was a line running from north-west of Steenstratt through Lizerne to a position southwest of

General Albrecht, Duke of Württemberg.

Pilckem, while XXVI Reserve Corps seized the high ground surrounding the road from Boesinghe to Langemarck, which extended to beyond German occupied Poelcapelle. The storming of a canal bridge and the seizure of the canal banks were a lesser objective. Only limited arrangements existed to exploit any success, for in his heart Falkenheyn doubted the gas attack would be a success.

The Kaiser's men realised that if they broke through at Steenstratt, itself the hinge of the Salient as well as the France-Belgian boundary, they would turn the inexperienced Canadians' flank. The beleaguered Canadians would have to retreat or fight an enemy to their front and rear. If the allies retreated to the canal, the majority of British troops from Broodseinde to near St Eloi would be cut off or forced to retreat through the shell-ravaged ruins of Ypres; but no allowance was made for Canadian grit.

The gas attack along Gravenstafel Ridge

On Thursday 22 April, a sunny morning, the lack of a favourable wind led to a postponement of the gas attack until the afternoon. German commanders, wary of attacking in broad daylight, were brusquely ordered, 'To advance and reach Hill 20 near Pilckem without fail'. The attack zone had been under fairly heavy shelling since the 19th for, unlike the British, the Germans did not suffer from a shortage of shells. Prior to 5 pm the guns ceased at the precise time the valves on the gas cylinders

Direction of the gas release.

facing the French 45th and 87th Divisions were opened. A steady northeasterly breeze wafted the toxic gases at a rate of six feet a second towards the French troops holding the Langemarck sector.

The French troops gazed in puzzlement at the strange apparition emanating from a considerable length of the German trenches. Jets of whiteish vapour swirled around until they settled into a compact low cloud bank, greenish brown below and yellow above, where it reflected the rays of the sinking sun. The ominous cloud, initially half a mile in depth, swiftly reached the French positions. Heavier than air, the deathly mist hugged the ground, pouring into trenches and engulfing the French and North African troops in its deadly vapour.

Like some liquid, the heavy vapour poured relentlessly into the trenches, filled them and passed on. For a few seconds nothing

Algerian troops in 1914.

happened; the sweet smelling stuff merely tickled their nostrils; they failed to realise the danger. Then, with inconceivable rapidity, the gas worked and blind panic spread. Hundreds, after a dreadful fight for air, became unconscious and died where they lay, a death of hideous torture, with the frothing bubbles gurgling in their throats and the foul liquid welling up in their lungs. With blackened faces and twisted limbs, one by one they drowned, only that which drowned them came from inside and not from out. Others, staggering, falling, lurching on and, of their ignorance keeping pace with the gas, went back. A hail of rifle and shrapnel mowed them down, and the line was broken.

Fifteen minutes after the gas was released the German infantry advanced. Sir Arthur Conan Doyle in his account of the 1915 campaign, wrote;

The French troops, staring over the top of their parapet at this curious screen, which ensured them a temporary relief from fire, were observed suddenly to throw up their hands, to clutch at their throats and to fall to the ground in the agonies of asphyxiation. Many lay where they had fallen, while their comrades, absolutely helpless against this diabolical agency, rushed madly out of the mephitic mist and made for the rear, over-running the lines of trenches behind them. Many of them never halted until they had reached Ypres, while others rushed westwards and put the canal between them and the enemy. The Germans, meanwhile, advanced and took possession of the successive lines of trenches, tenanted only by the dead garrisons, whose blackened faces, contorted figure and lips fringed with blood and foam from their bursting lungs, showed the agonies in which they died.

At 5.20 pm, five miles as the crow flies from the asphyxiating troops, the telephone rang at the Elverdinghe command centre, where Colonel Mordacq received the first of a spate of calls reporting gas and the evacuation of the front line. Evidently a man of action, he mounted a horse and rode hell for leather to Boesinghe, where he felt a violent tingling sensation in the nostrils and throat, his ears buzzed, breathing became painful and the pungent aroma of chlorine filled the air. Amid the chaos, men were in full flight, eyes streaming and behaving like mad men, bereft of their rifles and greatcoats, discarded to aid a speedier escape. They clamoured for water, some spat blood, while others trembled on the ground, gasping for air for their tortured lungs. Mordacq, in an attempt to halt the rout, ordered the 7th Zouaves, located just south of Boesinghe, to launch a counter attack across the canal. As the enemy advanced closer to the canal, Mordacq ordered a half battalion of the 2nd Zouaves to fall

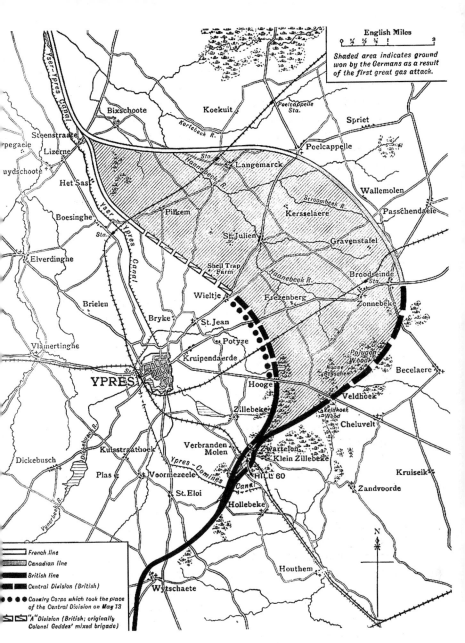

Shaded area indicates ground won by the Germans as a result of the first great gas attack.

The Salient before and after the gas attack.

back to the western canal bank and defend the bridges at Boesinghe. Meanwhile half-dazed Frenchmen fell back to the canal and established a line from Steenstratt to Boesinghe. Demolition charges were placed on the railway bridge south of the village in preparation for the expected

German incursion. The surviving half-dazed French fell back to the canal and established a line from Steenstratt to Boesinghe, itself threatened by the Germans. Throughout the night, enemy attempts to cross the canal at Boesinghe were repulsed but the enemy had driven a five-mile wide wedge into the line and penetrated to a depth of two miles; no defences existed between the eastern canal bank and the Canadian flank.

Rifleman Anthony R Hossack of 9/London Regiment (Queen Victoria's Rifles) was fresh from the fighting at Hill 60 and was now resting and awaiting an evening meal in a meadow off the Poperinghe - Ypres road. As the sun began to set, the noise of heavy shellfire from the direction of the French lines six-miles to the north-west became audible.

Rifleman Anthony R Hossack.

We could see in the failing light the flash of shrapnel and a curious low cloud of yellow–grey smoke, and underlying every thing a dull, confused murmuring. Suddenly down the road from the Yser canal came a galloping team of horses, the riders goading their mounts in a frenzied way; then another and another, till the road became a seething mass with a huge pall of dust over all. Plainly, something terrible was happening, but what was it? Officers, too, stood dumfounded, for in the northerly breeze came a pungent nauseating smell that tickled the throat and made our eyes smart. The horses and men were still pouring down the road, two or three men on a horse I saw, while over the fields streamed mobs of infantry, the dusky warriors of French Africa: away went their rifles, equipment, even their tunics, that they may run faster. One man came stumbling through our lines. An officer of ours held him up with a levelled revolver. "What's the matter, you bloody lot of cowards?" says he. The Zouave was frothing at the mouth, his eyes started from their sockets, and he fell writhing at the officer's feet.

By 6 pm Langemarck was in enemy hands, and gas enveloped the Canadian sector, prompting the completely outflanked Canadians to withdraw their left brigade back to the north of St Julian. Numerous acts of valour and self-sacrifice ensued among the Canadians, who determinedly stood their ground. Some French infantrymen, compelled to quit their ground by the gas, dashed towards the right and joined the

Canadians in battle. One was the commander of a battalion who the Canadians insisted should take command of his compatriots. He rallied the traumatised handfuls of Tirailleurs, Zouaves and Turcos and then shouted to them, 'Show these brave Canadians how French soldiers face death'. He died a soldier's death. The Canadians' brave stand undoubtedly prevented a demoralising retreat. A series of deadly attacks and costly counter attacks ensued within the Salient, Ypres was finally saved from capture. As the fighting to retain the town is beyond the remit of this book, the reader may wish to consult Battleground Ypres, *St Julien*, by Graham Keech.

Near Steenstraatt, the left of the 45th Reserve Division made slower progress. The gas was less effective and strong defensive fire from the formidable 75 mm field guns inflicted severe casualties on both the 45th and 46th Reserve Divisions. However, by late evening the 45th Division had entered the village of Steenstratt, crossed the canal near Het Sas and seized the neighbouring village of Lizerne. Throughout the night of 22/23 April, Allied counter attacks against Lizerne were beaten back by the Germans. The next day the 45th Reserve Division advanced and gained ground near the Yperlee stream, west of Steenstratt, but the advance lost impetus. Meanwhile, the advance of the 46th Reserve Division was halted by Allied reinforcements who had created defensive positions along the Lizerne-Boesinghe road.

On St George's Day, as the sun rose on the second day of the battle, Sir John French met with General Foch and they resolved to remove the enemy from their captured trenches. In time French reinforcements would arrive, meanwhile Sir John French agreed to despatch the Cavalry Corps to bolster the waning French numbers. Two British regular cavalry divisions were used: General Henry de Lisle's First Cavalry Division took up positions opposite Lizerne, whilst Sir Charles Kavanagh's 2nd Cavalry Division dismounted and joined the French territorial troops in the trenches forward of Boesinghe. Meanwhile, two brigades from III Corps and the Lahore Division of the Indian Army reinforced the Second Army. By eleven o'clock, the allied line ran from St Julien almost due west for a mile, then arched northward, reaching the canal near Boesinghe. Foch ordered Putz to hold his line, which was now the line of the canal, and prepare to counter attack the lost ground. That afternoon the French and Canadians advanced in the direction of Pilckem; no progress was made, but the Germans were stalled, allowing the dramatically altered front line to be patched up with exhausted and dazed survivors, whose numbers were increasingly boosted by the arrival of reinforcements.

Among the reinforcements was a medical officer of 1 Brigade

Canadian Artillery, who had previously served in the Canadian artillery as a lieutenant during the Boer War. In peacetime he was a lecturer in pathology but he rejoined the artillery at the onset of war. McCrae later served as a surgeon and secured lasting fame in the sector he now approached; he was to die of pneumonia before the war's end.

John McCrae.

Early on Friday 23 April, we received forty-five minutes notice to support a French counter attack scheduled for 4.30 am. We took to the road at once, going at full gallop, taking up a position along the Yser canal. We were to the left of the British line and behind French troops, a position we [the guns] remained at for seventeen days. We got into action at once, under heavy shellfire, and immediately began to register our guns, and almost at once had to get into steady firing on a large sector of the front. We dug in the guns as quickly as we could, and took as our headquarters some infantry trenches already sunk on a ridge near the canal. We were subject from the first to a steady and accurate shelling, for we were all but in sight, as were the German trenches 2,000 yards to our front. At times, the fire would come in salvos quickly repeated. Bursts of fire would be made for ten or fifteen minutes at a time. We got all sorts of projectiles, from three inch to eight inch, or perhaps ten inch; the small ones usually as air bursts, the larger percussion and air, and the heaviest percussion only...So the day went on. Three different German attacks were made and repulsed....

On 24 April, he graphically described his surroundings. His censored description relates to the steeply banked canal bounded by the Ypres to Boesinghe road. The road bridge to the east of Brielen was Number Four Bridge, constructed in military fashion using sturdy timber trestles, the centre trestle resting on a stranded canal barge.

Behold us now anything less than two miles north of Ypres on the west bank of the canal. This runs north, each bank flanked with high elms, with bare trunks of the familiar Netherlands type. A few yards to the west a main road runs, likewise bordered. The Censor will allow me to say that on the high bank between these we had our headquarters. The ridge is perhaps fifteen to twenty feet high, and

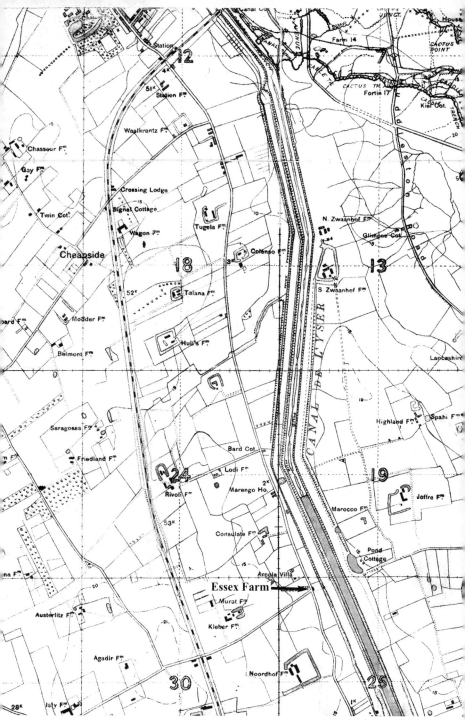

The Canal north of Ypres, from the Essex Farm (arrowed) area to the southern outskirts of Boesinghe.

slopes forward fifty yards to the water. The back is steeper and
slopes quickly to a little subsidiary waterway, deep but dirty. Where
the guns are I shall not say; but they were not far away, and the
German aeroplanes that viewed us daily with all but impunity knew
very well. A road crossed over the canal and interrupted the ridge;
across the road from us was our billet the place we cooked in, at
least, and where we usually took our meals. Looking to the south,
between the trees, we could see the ruins of Ypres, to the front on
the sky line, with rolling ground in the front, pitted by French
trenches, the German lines, to the left front, several farms and a
windmill, and further left, again near the canal, thicker trees and
more farms. The farms and windmills were soon burnt. Several
farms we used for observing posts were also quickly burnt during
the next three or four days. All along behind us at varying distances
were French and British guns; their flashes at night light up the sky.
These high trees were at once a protection and a danger. Shells that
struck them were usually destructive. When we came in the foliage
was still very thin. Along the road, which was constantly shelled 'on
spec' by the Germans, one saw all the sights of war; wounded men,
limping or carried, ambulances, trains of supply, troops, army
mules and tragedies. I saw one bicycle orderly, a shell exploded and
he seemed to pedal on for eight or ten revolutions and then
collapsed in a heap – dead. Straggling soldiers would be killed or
wounded, horses also, until it got to be a nightmare. I used to
shudder every time I saw wagons or troops on that road.

The dressing station took the form of a timber dug out burrowed into the
foot of the canal bank. According to McCrae's superior, Lieutenant
Colonel Morrison, during the battle shot men rolled down the bank into
the dressing station. A few hundred yards distant, by a regimental
headquarters, was the nucleus of today's Essex Farm cemetery. On
Sunday 25 April Major John McCrae noted:

Today we got our dressing-station dug out complete, and we slept
there at night. Three farms in succession burned on our front –
colour in the otherwise dark. The shells flashed over the front and
rear in all directions. The city was still burning and the procession
still going on. I dressed a number of French wounded; one Turco
prayed to Allah and Mohamed all the time I was dressing his wound.
On the front field one can see the dead lying here and there, and in
places where an assault has been they lie very thick on the forward
slopes of the German trenches.

The Belgians retook Lizerne on 27 April, after a bombardment followed
by a charge of Belgian infantry and Zouaves. Six German guns were

Belgian defenders clash with the invader on the banks of the Yser.

captured, and the Belgians and their comrades swept forward towards Het Sas, evicting the enemy from his first line of trenches. On 15 May, the Zouaves and Algerian sharpshooters of General Putz captured a trench on the fringe of Steenstratt, then stormed the village and reached the canal bank. Approximately 600 German corpses were reputed to be around the village. Meanwhile, a fierce Belgian bombardment destroyed enemy

The wrecked village of Lizerne.

Lieutenant General Horace Smith-Dorrien.

Lieutenant General Herbert Plumer.

positions; 'we entered the village with our hands in our pockets', claimed a Zouave. Despite extensive use of artillery, German counter attacks all failed. By 17 May, excluding wounded or prisoners, no Germans remained on the west canal bank. The French had avenged their poisoned comrades by retaking three villages and their defensive infrastructure.

Meanwhile at the British front Lieutenant General Smith-Dorrien, the commander of Second Army, became increasingly pessimistic about the value of the morale sapping and seemingly futile counter attacks and, with the improbability of French co-operation, recommended a withdrawal from the Salient. After writing to Robertson, the Chief of the General Staff, requesting that Sir John French review operations in the Salient, he was rebuked. Despite making an accurate assessment of the situation, he was replaced by Lieutenant General Plumer, whose first orders were to carry out the withdrawal proposed by his predecessor. The most difficult phase of the operation was the final one, when on the night of 2/3rd May most of the artillery had to fall back across the canal.

At 4 pm on 2 May, the Germans tried unsuccessfully to breach the line between Boesinghe and Zonnebeke by a further gas release, during which the Canadians suffered greatly. The maelstrom of scything shrapnel and high explosive shells claimed another insignificant soul when a shell burst killed McCrae's good friend and former student, twenty-two year old Lieutenant Alexis Hannan Helmer. Soldiers with sand bags collected the remains of the Second Battery, Royal Canadian Artillery, officer. They arranged them on an army blanket, secured with safety pins, in preparation for an interment under the protective cloak of darkness. That evening, in the absence of the chaplain, McCrae conducted the funeral service. Already physically drained from treating a seemingly unending stream of casualties, it is reputed (accounts do differ) that the grief stricken McCrae sat on the step of an ambulance and hastily composed a piece of poetry. The amateur poet, who wrote only twenty-eight indifferent poems prior to the Great War and two in wartime, was unimpressed with his verse, McCrae flung his draft away,

A burial party, engaged in burying corpses and fragments of corpses wrapped in army blankets, pause for a camera to record the event.

An early attempt at providing protection against gas attack – a chemically treated flannel pad and goggles.

but Colonel Morrison recovered it and forwarded the poem to the *Spectator* magazine. It rejected the poem, but on 8 December 1915 *Punch* published McCrae's poem '*In Flanders Fields*', which rapidly achieved enormous popularity. Shortly afterwards, probably as a consequence of his new-found fame and much to his annoyance, McCrae received a transfer to Number Three (McGill) Canadian General Hospital, where he took up the position of Chief of Medical Services.

The Battle of Second Ypres ground to a halt in late May. The Germans failed to break through or capture the exalted prize of Ypres, but the cost was over 59,000 British, Indian and Canadian casualties.

Boesinghe church 1915. The gradual destruction of the church reflects the destruction inflicted on the village.

Chapter Three

FRONT LINE BOESINGHE JUNE-JULY 1915

Following the gas release, the advancing German infantry witnessed the horrific deaths of the French opposition. Not wishing to experience the same fate as their adversary, they were extremely reluctant to advance in the wake of the poison gas. This understandable fear of the new weapon undoubtedly cost Germany a much more significant victory and indeed reflects a major lost opportunity. However, near Boesinghe, overcoming determined resistance, the enemy gained ground, despite later being forced back to the eastern canal bank by the troops of General Putz. The Flemish village, previously a couple of miles behind the front, now had the enemy on the opposite canal bank. The German line extended along the canal edge for a few hundred yards south of the railway embankment, the front line then arched eastwards, holding the enemy at bay in positions that would remain unaltered for over two years. The German blows after the battle drew to a close were now concentrated elsewhere and a period of relative inactivity descended upon the sector, for both the French and Germans appear to have adopted a policy of 'live and let live' here.

Consequently, little of note occurred until the first week of June 1915, when the 4th Division, comprising regular and reservist troops, transferred from V Corps to the newly created VI Corps, under the command of Lieutenant General Sir John L Keir; it was joined by the 6th Division from III Corps.

The 4th Division had fought in most of the major battles of 1914 and during the recent fighting had sustained heavy losses northeast of Ypres. The depleted Division, situated near Armentières, close to the Franco-Belgian border, now relocated once more to the northern end of the Salient. On the night of 7 and 8 June 1915, the Division began the relief of the French and the British took up positions whose line extended from (and including) Turco Farm to a point on the Yser Canal approximately 600 yards south of Boesinghe Bridge; the entire Salient was now in British hands.

As with most French trenches, the line did not meet British standards, especially as regards sanitation. Trenches originally built by the enemy and subsequently taken by the French were in an appalling state of squalor and decomposing enemy corpses littered the area, giving off a pervading air of death. *The History of the Black Watch* records: 'Apparently, the sector had been a peaceful one when occupied by the French, judging by the way they lived in wooden huts in the front line....'

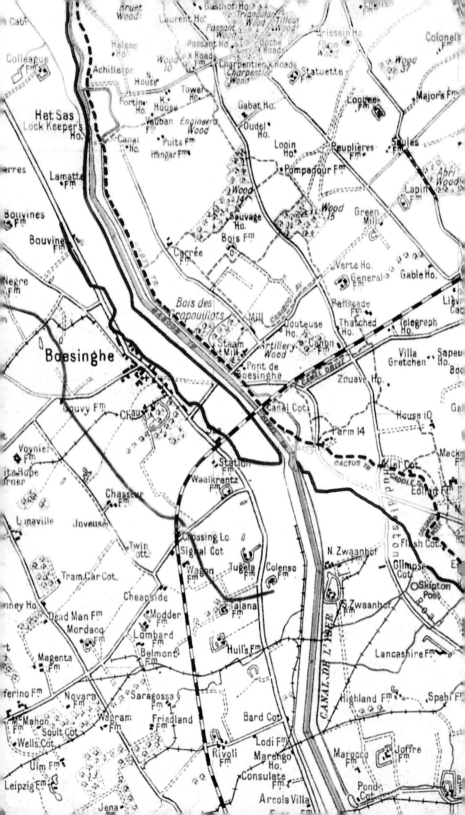

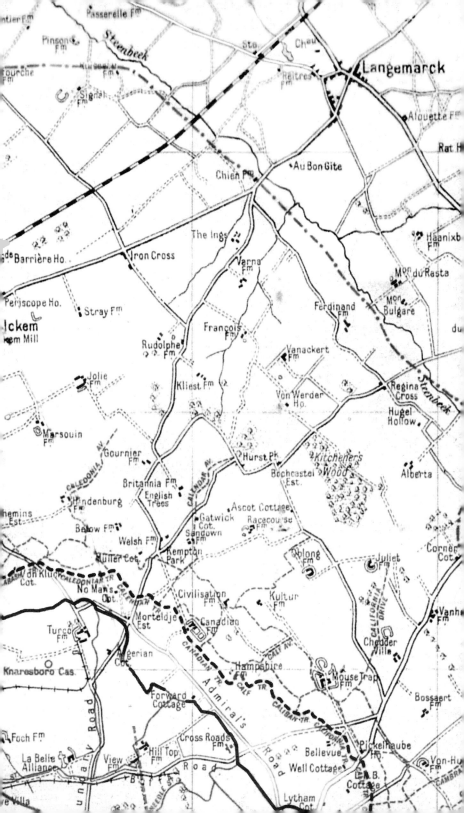

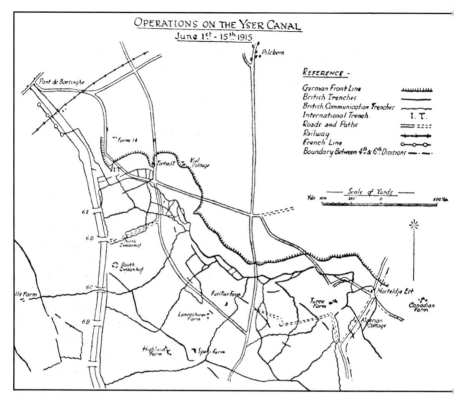

Reference –

German Front Line
British Trenches
British Communication Trenches
International Trench. I. T.
Roads and Paths
Railway
French Line
Boundary Between 4th & 6th Divisions

Scale of Yards

The British initiated a complete overhaul of the defences, supplemented by new dug outs, machine-gun and mortar positions. These labours were fraught with danger. For example, between 21 to 25 June, when 2/Hampshires were in the line, on a particularly dark night that helped to conceal their activity, A and B companies excavated a new forward trench close to the enemy. Their labours were warmly praised by the authorities, but the battalion sustained four dead and thirty-eight wounded in the process. These figures might not be excessive, for Sir Herbert Plumer, commanding Second Army, said he was pleased if his casualties did not exceed 200 a day while employed in ordinary trench work.

Beneath the Flanders plain a thick belt of blue alluvial clay acts as a barrier to the absorption of surface water, resulting in a high water table two or three feet below the spongy soil's surface. Throughout the Salient and in the Boesinghe sector, the construction of fieldworks proved problematic. The geology was unsuitable for trenches, which soon became water-filled ditches; and the misery the troops endured in such appalling conditions would be duly noted by a succession of battalion war diarists. The field engineering difficulties were further compounded by the close proximity of the enemy. The construction and maintenance of the trench infrastructure was unending. Due to the danger, most of this work occurred during the hours of darkness when troops, ostensibly resting, were assigned to Royal Engineer fatigue parties. Some of the trenches, hastily dug in the heat of battle, were found to be badly positioned, so were abandoned; others were incorporated into the new system. Where it proved impossible to run a continuous front line, a series of isolated outlying pickets or 'grouse butts' were constructed. They afforded a meagre protection to their occupants, for the posts only had sandbag and hurdle walls surmounted by a roof of corrugated iron clad with sandbags or earth; and were usually only accessible over ground in the hours of darkness. The depth of the trenches was determined by the water table; consequently a ditch of two or three feet depth might be revetted with corrugated iron or sandbag walls to a height adequate for a man to stand upright. Walls built from two courses of sandbags provided protection against shrapnel, shell splinters and small arms fire. The earthen banks flanking the canal were honeycombed with dugouts, which were gradually transformed into billets, medical posts, stores and headquarters. Given their proximity to the front line, these were a far from safe billet and were only used by the companies in immediate reserve to the companies holding the line.

The Yser Canal formed a chord through the rear of the Salient, and

A sketch map of bridges and front line sections.

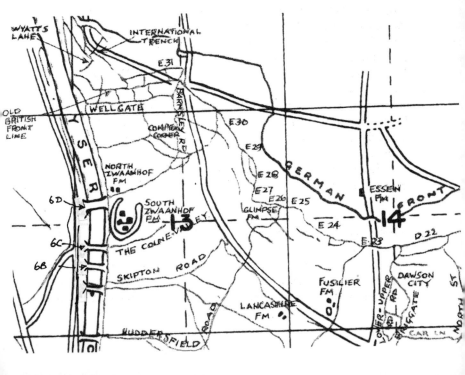

thus hampered the forward movement of all troops and logistics. Across this watery divide, British and Canadian engineering companies threw crossings, most of which only at the very limit of the imagination could merit the description 'bridge'. Some, constructed from barrels or petrol cans fastened together beneath a deck of assorted timbers, offered a precarious and usually wet passage across the canal. The structures were identified by a letter and number; only a couple merited a name. Enemy artillery regularly destroyed the flimsy structures, which engineers then rebuilt overnight. A 1915 diagram shows eleven crossings between Halifax Road communication trench and Boesinghe Railway Bridge. Serving the northern part of the Zwanhoff Farm sector was the spindly Bridge 6D, also referred to as Blighty Bridge. This was a tongue in cheek euphemism, for rarely did anyone hit whilst crossing the bridge return home. Brielen, or Number 4 Bridge, was the only structure capable of withstanding traffic and each night men and trucks incessantly crossed back and forth over it. A further hive of activity existed on the western bank of the canal at Bridge 6, the location of the Royal Engineer and main supply dumps. Each night, amid scenes of apparent chaos, carrying parties, ration parties and wiring parties converged on the dump, negotiating their way past roaring trucks, mules and horse drawn wagons.

The enemy held the east canal bank facing Boesinghe to approximately 250 yards south of the railway bridge. A distance of seventy-five yards separated the German and British trenches, whilst the French boundary commenced on the west bank. Wiring was impossible due to the proximity of the enemy, so ready made *cheveaux de frise* barriers consisting of two X shaped supports spaced by a stout length of timber, acting as a framework for coiled barbed wire, were pushed out from the trench over the parapet. To prevent enemy infiltration into the rear of the British line, the east canal bank near No Man's Land was fenced with similar barricades. The British line ran parallel with the canal bank for approximately 450 yards before turning acutely to the east for a further 400 yards, where another sharp right turn took the line in a southerly direction towards Turco Farm, which served as the dividing line between 4th and 6th Divisional sectors. The German-held heights overlooked all the trenches and their rear infrastructure.

To the south of Zwanhof Farm, the enemy forward line was a few hundred yards from the canal bank; sandwiched between their front and the canal stood the trenches of the extreme left post of the British line. An officer wrote:

> To this post the garrison and visitor usually marched, as Napolean said of every army, 'on its belly', but when a good trench made it accessible to a general of high rank it aroused in him great

Knife rest barricades in place on the banks of the canal, defending the rear of British trenches at Boesinghe at the northen point of the Ypres Salient.

Trench map detail showing part of the village of Boesinghe and the northern end of the Salient.

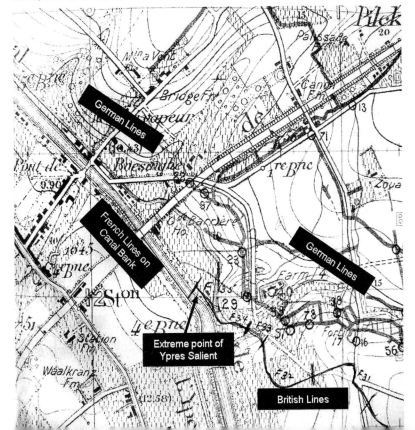

enthusiasm. It was, for him, the left post of the left platoon of the left company of the left division of the left corps of the British Army, and he warmly shook the platoon commander by the hand and congratulated him on this great post. The platoon commander, on the retirement of the general, inquired of the sentry if he had listened to the general, and realised the importance of his situation. The sentry said 'Yes'. Thereupon the platoon commander gravely said 'Then if you receive the order 'British Army – Left form', you, sentry, will make a smart turn to the left and mark time till the end of the war!

The troops sandwiched into this area were in an unenviable position, enfiladed from the left flank and swept by fire from the defences upon Pilckem Ridge. Facing this narrow foothold of territory was a shallow enemy salient, fronted by International Trench, a name reputed to refer to the number of times the trench changed nationalities. This trench, initially constructed by the French, but now in German possession, was significantly improved during May and June 1915.

A small but successful operation; International Trench June-July 1915

On 17 June, Second Army headquarters notified VI Corps it was required to attack the south end of International Trench to a point 350 yards to the north to improve the tactical position. General Plumer also wanted to distract the enemy's attention from an intended operation due to be imminently launched at Hooge. Approximately 350 yards east of the trench was a fist shaped earthwork, *Fortin* 17 (French for a small temporary field defence, designated 17), supported by a heavy trench mortar. This obstacle needed to be eliminated before an attack on the ruins of Ferme 14 (a farm sited on a hillock fourteen metres above sea level). Roughly 600 yards to the rear lay the German second line, supported by artillery and machine guns dispersed along Pilckem Ridge.

During the French occupancy of the sector, Colonel Dechissele of the Zouaves, had conceived a plan to capture *Fortin* 17 and this now provided the basis for a small scale British attack. The proposed attack had prompted a debate between the staff at VI Corps and the 4th Division's commander (Wilson) who, aware of the Division's losses and the shortage of trained officers and men, was reluctant to attempt anything substantial. Instead of attacking the whole Salient between *Ferme* 14 and *Fortin* 17, yet obliged to meet the Army Commander's orders, Keir prepared an attack on International Trench, scheduled for 6 July.

Meanwhile, German artillery and snipers attempted to make the northern limit of the British line untenable. Effective retaliation proved difficult, for at this time British hand grenades were still in the experimental stage and few men had been trained in their use. Furthermore, artillery ammunition was still in short supply and the few shells made available for *Fortin* 17 merely aggravated the Germans, who responded with fierce retaliatory bombardments. Under this remorseless shelling, British casualties steadily mounted during the thirty days of

Ferme 14, situated behind International Trench, contained a German heavy trench mortar. Pilkem Ridge can be seen on the skyline.

June. The 1/East Lancashire's alone incurred losses of four officers wounded, twenty-eight other ranks killed in action, six others died of their wounds, another man died probably through illness and ninety-eight other ranks were wounded.

Danger came in other ways as well. During late June, German sappers began excavating a sap from International Trench towards the canal; their intention appeared to be the detonation of a mine beneath the British front

The action at International Trench 6 July 1915.

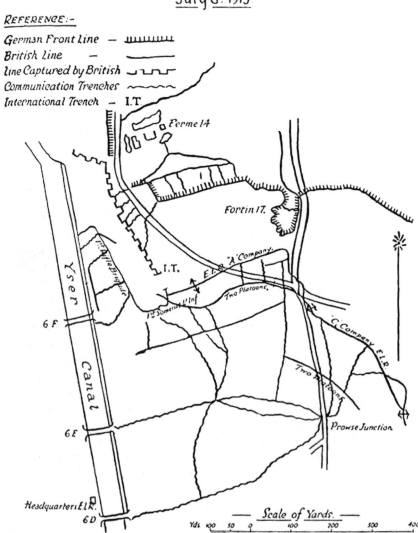

line. To eliminate the threat, the British launched a minor operation on Sunday, 4 July. Prior to the raid, howitzer shells rained down on the enemy trench, fortuitously destroying a well placed machine gun. A platoon of 2/Seaforth Highlanders successfully advanced to cover a Royal Engineer party detailed to destroy the tunnel. The few Germans who survived the bombardment were driven out with the bayonet. The Royal Engineers sank a fifteen-foot deep hole, which they charged with 200 pounds of explosives; the resulting explosion destroyed the sap. As they worked, they were shielded by men like Private R Miller, whose DCM citation reads:

> Private Miller, immediately on entering the German saphead, pushed forward with a non-commissioned officer up a communication trench and prevented the German bombing party from getting within range of the Royal Engineer detachment destroying the sap. After the non-commissioned officer had been wounded, he remained at his post alone until the whole of the storming party had been withdrawn.

Second Lieutenant George S Rawstone received the Military Cross for showing 'the greatest dash in carrying out this difficult task, and finally, although wounded, carrying out the withdrawal most satisfactorily'.

The battle for International Trench

It was decided to cancel the the operation at Hooge; but the, arguably futile, 6 July attack by 11 Brigade was to go ahead, fronted by 1/Rifle Brigade with 1/Somerset Light Infantry in support. Over two nights Second Lieutenant William P A Robinson, of 135 Battery Royal Field Artillery, and Lieutenant Robert L Withington, 9 Field Company Royal Engineers, (both received the MC) supervised the movement of an eighteen-pounder gun over the canal to destroy another saphead in International Trench. To reach its destination the gun was hauled over the high canal embankment, rafted over the canal, itself under fire, dragged up the opposite bank, a slope of forty-five degrees, then over three trenches and a skyline to its position in a prepared gun pit sited within seventy-yards of the German line. Field Marshal Sir John French cited the incident in his dispatch of 15 October 1915 as: *An example of the difficulties which his officers and men were constantly called upon to overcome, and of the spirit of initiative and resource which animated them throughout the campaign.*

On the eve of the attack, men from two companies of the 1/East Lancashires dug communication trenches including one from Bridge 6D to Hulls Farm. The latter new trench was used extensively on the first day of the battle and over the next few days a steady procession of wounded trod its muddy path.

An hour before zero, British and French artillery commenced their bombardment of International Trench, accompanied by the 18-pounder firing over open sights with devastating effect, blowing up the sap and some thirty yards of thick wire entanglement. In response, a counter barrage fell on the assembly trench, inflicting the first casualties. At 6.00 am two companies from 1/Rifle Brigade advanced across the fifty yards of No Man's Land; to their right, A Company of the East Lancashires provided heavy rifle and machine gun fire, supplemented by the new

A war diary sketch map detailing the 1/East Lancashires' preparations for attack.

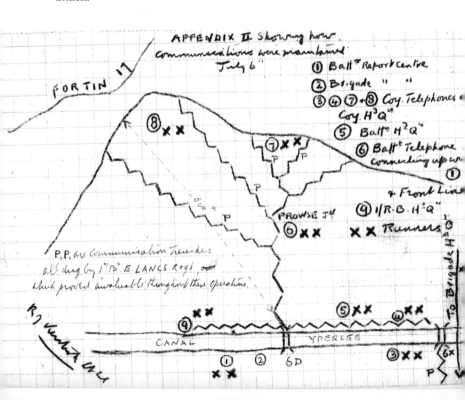

Another view of Ferme 14.

Mills bombs (hand grenades). The destroyed wire no longer barred the way, allowing the Rifle Brigade to pour into the German line and bombers began a lengthy battle with their opposite numbers. On either flank of the captured 500 yards of International Trench fierce bombing fights commenced. Thirty minutes into the attack, shells destroyed bridges 6 and 6D, requiring the engineers to begin bridge repairs under shellfire. About this time heavy shelling badly damaged the trench held by A Company, killing almost a platoon of 1/East Lancashires, whilst they also lost twenty-men men from C Company when a reserve trench to the south was demolished. Meanwhile 1/Somerset Light Infantry had advanced in support of the Rifle Brigade. One company occupied the western support trench; two other companies, in conjunction with the Royal Engineers, proceeded to create new fire and communication trenches. By 7.30 am, they had reached a depth of three feet, but sustained forty per cent casualties from sniper and shellfire. At 7.30, as well, the enemy attempted to advance from the left, but artillery checked them. By late morning the relief of depleted sections of men began. At 1.00 pm the enemy laid a heavy bombardment on the British front, support and communication trenches. However, an hour later a determined two hour bombing onslaught on the flanks of the captured trenches failed to remove the

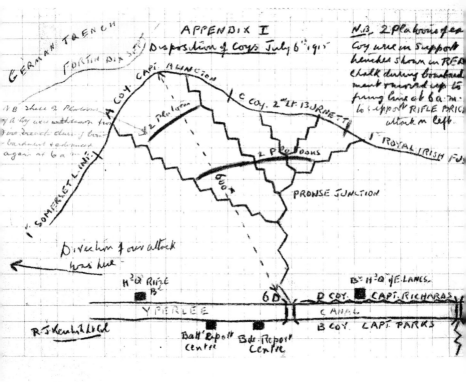

Sketch from the 1/EastLancashire War Diary showing unit dispositions.

brigade bombers and the Somerset Light Infantry. At 3 pm, the enemy had gathered on the left in readiness for another counter attack, but artillery broke this up.

Two companies of the Hampshire Regiment, which had come up in support, now helped defend the new trench. At 3.30 the captured trench and the temporarily evacuated original British line were heavily shelled. Once more the enemy advanced from the left, this time using a communication trench; artillery stemmed the advance but British shells firing short landed among the Somersets. Second Lieutenant C A Gould of the Somersets arrived to find a devastated trench and the saphead defended by only three bombers. He and Sergeant Burston joined in the fight while the rest of his platoon worked feverishly on the trench, successfully reversing the parapet. Shortly after 5 pm the bombardment became intermittent, eventually ceasing two hours before midnight. Overnight the gun from 135th Battery was withdrawn, the Rifle Brigade were relieved by 2/Lancashire Fusiliers, and the Somersets by 1/Royal Warwicks, who spent the next four days and nights defending the newly gained territory.

Around thirty Germans became prisoners, the majority belonging to the 215th Regiment; but some of the captives belonged to the 213th, in support; both were Landsturm regiments from Schleswig-Holstein and were reputed to have had only four months' training. The British also captured two machine guns, two trench mortars and various trench stores.

The cost in human terms of seventy-five yards of ground over a 300 yard frontage gained in this 'small but successful operation' comprised, 1/Somerset Light Infantry: Second Lieutenant Webber and twenty-seven other ranks killed, with a further 102 wounded. Second Lieutenants Trent, Stead and Edwards were wounded. The Rifle Brigade lost Second Lieutenants Blair, George Francis Juckes, Bernard Gibbs MC, and Lieutenant Douglas Robert Brandt, the latter dying of wounds. *Soldiers Died in the Great War* lists sixty-seven other ranks killed; of these seven were former lancers. The wounded included Captains Downes and Ellis, Second Lieutenants Bullocks and Doyle and 176 other ranks. The 1/East Lancashire casualty return from 5th to 7 July records one officer and forty-two other ranks killed, six officers and 195 other ranks wounded. The 1/East Lancashires Commanding Officer, Lieutenant Colonel R J Kentish, later attributed approximately ninety per cent of the battalions casualties to at least eighteen heavy calibre guns shelling 11 Brigade sector.

4697 Private H Bramall 1/East Lancashire KIA 9 July 1915 Grave II D 7 Talana Farm Cemetery.

On the night of 8/9 July two companies from the Hampshires relieved the East Lancashires; A and D companies occupied the front line, where they were heavily shelled, while bombing duels went on all day. One officer wrote, 'We had an awful time, my company was in the worst place in all the line, and they shelled us the whole time'. Nevertheless, the battalion held the badly damaged trenches; but, as the parapet was far from bullet proof, eighteen men died and fifty-five received wounds. For example, Captain Gwynne, the battalion medical officer for almost a year, was employed dressing the wounds of Lancashire Fusiliers in the front line. On hearing that a Rifle Brigade man, badly wounded three days earlier, was lying out in a half dug trench, he went to his aid. After bandaging the wounds of the rifleman, Captain Gwynne was hit in the head and died. Captain John Fitzgerald Gwynne MC, RAMC, died on 9 July, aged twenty-six. This Sheffield officer lies in Talana farm Cemetery II D 16.

On 10 July, after a heavy bombardment, the enemy re-captured their former positions from the 5/York and Lancaster who promptly counter attacked and re-captured the lost ground.

In keeping with usual practice, units constantly rotated between the front and rear areas, ensuring that a procession of battalions served in this inhospitable stretch of the line. There were no regrets when, a couple of days after the International Trench action, the 4th Division received orders to move south to the comparatively quiet Somme region; they would be relieved by the territorial battalions of the 49th (West Riding) Division.

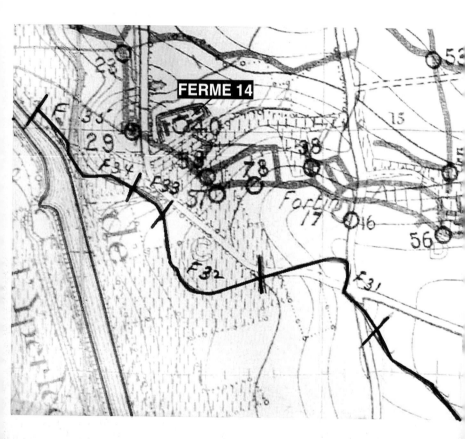

Chapter Four

THE 49TH (WEST RIDING) TERRITORIAL
DIVISION IN THE LINE: JULY-DECEMBER 1915

Soldiers approaching the northerly sector of the Salient almost inevitably passed through the sprawling market town of Poperinghe, where shrapnel once regularly rattled upon the cobblestones. 'Pop', as it was affectionately known, was the forward base for the Ypres Salient and the *Mairie* (or Town Hall) usually accommodated a divisional headquarters. The narrow cobbled streets were thronged with khaki clad figures snatching precious hours' leave and generally living life as if there were no tomorrow. Some gleefully headed for the frequently bombarded railway station to catch a leave train, while weary, mud-caked battalions wound their way towards the hop house next to the station. The brewers had long departed and the three great beer vats now served as army bathtubs. Once freshly scrubbed and clean clothed the other rankers disposed of their meagre wages in the cinema, numerous cafes and estaminets, or less salubrious venues; the officers' patronised genteel establishments such as Skindles. On a street at the square, a 6th Division chaplain Neville Talbot instituted the renowned Toc H, where every man

Troops passing through in Poperinghe square. The Maison de Ville estaminet was eventually destroyed by shellfire.

was equal regardless of rank. Over ninety years after first opening its doors the premises continues to attract thousands of battlefield visitors.

Three miles east of the town, in Coppernolle Woods, stood Number One Rest Camp, which became very familiar to the Yorkshire Territorials. The men were billeted fifteen to a tent, route marches and parades were minimal and many a weary Salient soldier recuperated from his exertions there or received a leave pass.

Elverdinghe Chateau in peacetime.

On leaving the town, troops destined for the extreme left flank of the British line headed for the heavily bombarded village of Elverdinghe. They travelled along a road which snaked its way through old hop fields, occasionally dotted with clusters of military graves. A light railway evacuated casualties from Elverdinghe to Poperinghe and consequently the fatally wounded were interred in the expanding cemeteries in and around the market town. On the return trip, the light railway carried supplies to the army camps, medical centres and stores scattered about Elverdinghe. The village boasted a grand chateau, which now served as advanced army headquarters, being approximately one and a half miles to the rear of the Boesinghe front. The chateau stood within its own ornamental park, screened from observers up on Pilckem Ridge by a belt of trees. To the rear and sides, a thick wood embraced the chateau and provided good cover for wooden billets constructed beneath the trees. In addition, nine other camps were situated within a one mile radius of the chateau. Popular opinion claimed that as long as British artillery refrained from shelling Pilckem Chateau the Germans would respect Elverdinghe Chateau. However this owed its charmed existence to more than a pact with the enemy. Within the well-wooded park, various cavalry squadrons dug deep and sturdy trenches, creating a veritable strong post. The infantry scathingly suggested the troopers might be more meaningfully employed furnishing working parties to the second line in front of Talana Farm, while *they* took a turn digging in the park. While the chateau received little damage, artillery destroyed the village. Troops in reserve removed the house bricks to form the base for horse-lines and shelters for Brigade Transports.

During April 1915, the 49th Division had proceeded overseas to serve its apprenticeship in the front line in IV Corps sector at Fleurbaix, south of Armentières. An assessment of the Division appears in correspondence

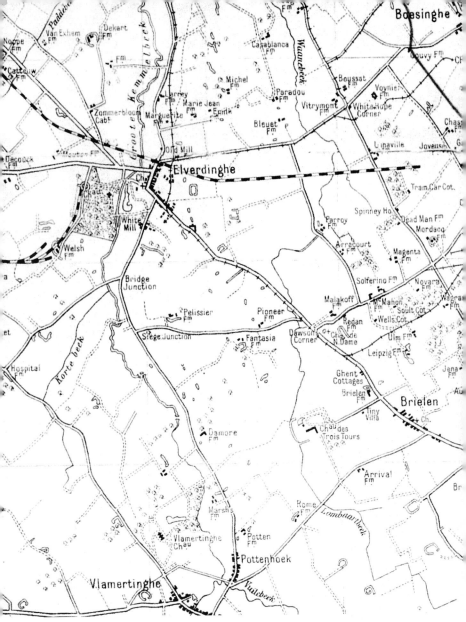

Rest area around the village of Elverdinghe. Whilst the village suffered destruction the Germans respected the Chateau and surrounding wood.

from Sir Henry Rawlinson to Lord Kitchener, dated 21 April 1915.

...The West Yorkshire Division is certainly a fine lot of men with a very fair lot of brigade commanding officers, but the staff is a bit weak. We shall have to lend them some staff officers who know their

jobs. At present, I am gradually introducing officers and non commissioned officers, as well as a proportion of the men, into the arts of trench warfare. They go down and spend twenty-four hours at a time in the trenches alongside the regular battalion now holding them and in this way gradually pick up the tricks of the trade. Baldock, who commands the division, is rather long in the tooth but he has good experience and if we can get him to understand the practical side of soldiering he will do all right. At present, he is much too addicted to theory, but this I hope will vanish when he finds himself face to face with the Germans.

The 49th Division transferred to First Army at the end of May. A month later, after a gratifying endorsement from Sir Douglas Haig, the division was re-transferred from the First Army, Indian Corps to the Second Army, VI Corps. During the first week of July the division moved to Proven, north-west of Poperinghe, from where they passed through the deserted and much knocked about village of Elverdinghe and gradually entered the canal sector.

The 49th Division was the first Territorial division assigned a long spell in the Ypres Salient. Their orders were simple and to the point, 'To hold at all costs, and not a single inch of ground was to be lost'. The divisional frontage reached from the east bank of the Yser canal near Boesinghe to Morteldje Estaminet on the Ypres-Langemarck Road, a

Major General T S Baldock CB. front of two and a half miles. The French 45th Division was to the left of the British Territorials while on their right flank were the troops of the 6th Division.

The division now received its first taste of trench mortars, against which it had no effective counter. The few British ammunition manufacturers were slow to gear up to the demands of modern warfare and were at the time incapable of supplying sufficient shells in either quality or quantity. The issue became a national scandal after Loos, but in the meantime (according to the 1/6th West Yorks regimental history) the 49th Division artillery had only three dozen fifteen pounder guns and a ration of three shells per gun per day. On the extreme left of the line the British were grateful for the presence of the French seventy-fives, which consistently came to the aid of their neighbour.

Two 49th Division officers with a German trench mortar captured in the fighting near Boesinghe.

First days in the line, commencing 9 July 1915

148 Brigade (3rd West Riding) took up positions at the northern most part of the line, 147 Brigade held the centre and 146 Brigade the right. The first of the Yorkshiremen into the front line were 1/5 York and Lancaster, whose war diarist noted on 9 July 1915:

> *Evening march via Elverdinghe to the Yser Canal, where the battalion took over trenches on the left of the British line, recently captured from the Germans by 11 Brigade near Boesinghe. Relief completed by 1.30 am on the morning of 10 July. The trenches taken over by the battalion were in a terrible state. Several of them had only recently been captured from the Germans and very little had been done to consolidate the position. A large number of dead were still unburied, both of our own [and] of the enemy and the conditions in which the officers and men had to live were terrible. The trenches and canal bank were strewn with rifles and equipment belonging to killed and wounded of the units previously in occupation of the line and with ammunition, bombs and stores of every description. These were collected as far as possible and depots formed at different points. A number of men re-armed themselves with SMLE rifles and*

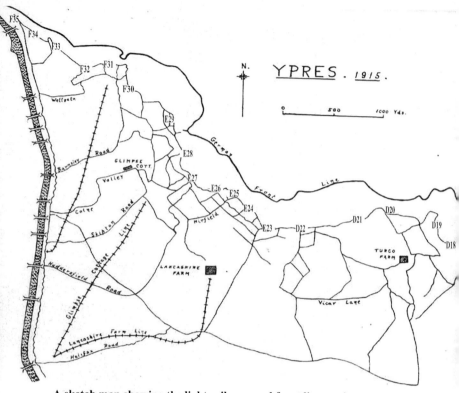

A sketch map showing the light railways and front line section numbers.

long bayonets in place of their CLLE rifles and short bayonets. [The 1895 Long Lee Enfield Mark 1 rifles were modified in 1907 to allow loading with a five round charger clip, hence the name Charger Loading Lee Enfield. The SMLE adopted in 1902 already had this facility and became the standard British infantry weapon of both world wars.]

The battalion was disposed thus: A Company held the right flank; B Company were in the centre and held a forward trench on the Pilckem Road; D Company were on the left flank along the east canal bank; the French were on the left on the west canal bank. C Company were in support of the centre on the canal bank and headquarters were located on the west bank, close to Bridge 6D, opposite South Zwaanhof Farm.

During the whole of the day, [10 July] *the trenches were heavily bombarded by the enemy and the parapets blown in several places. The machine gun was overturned and buried together with most of the team, one of whom was killed and one wounded. The casualties for this period were heavy, amounting to twenty-seven other ranks killed in action, Captain Stephen Rhodes and 127 other ranks wounded and two others missing.*

Argyll and Sutherland Highlanders in the Bois Grenier sector wearing gas masks issued 3 May 1915.

The next day the depleted battalion, upon relief by 1/4 (Hallamshire) York and Lancaster, proceeded to Elverdinghe Chateau. They endured steady shelling throughout the day, in trenches littered with English and German dead. The enemy now used shells to deliver toxic or irritant gases and, on 13 July, the Hallamshires endured hundreds of tear gas shells. A lack of wind prevented the dispersion of the gas and, after a twenty-minute bombardment, the British artillery replied. The enemy commenced rapid rifle fire before they advanced towards the British, but the severity of the barrage made their advance impossible. Within two days the Hallamshire battalion suffered three officers wounded (one fatally) and seventy-two other ranks killed or wounded. Shrapnel from the British guns caused several of these casualties, mainly due to the

Retailers stocked items for the public to buy and forward to their loved ones in the trenches. This gas mask was available from a Paris retailer prior to August 1915.

shells hitting the trees on the west bank of the canal.

Throughout the Salient, decomposing corpses, and the debris of a hundred small battles littered, the gas-contaminated terrain. Persistent shelling continued throughout each miserable day and snipers located in buildings at the east end of Boesinghe Bridge, with a half-mile field of fire along the canal bank, proved troublesome. Enemy machine guns positioned to the north of the British also enfiladed some of the canal crossings. Conditions were further aggravated by the enemy's use of lachrymatory (tear gas) shells. From Pilckem Ridge observers were able to direct fire on any likely target; the 1/5 and 1/4 (Hallamshire) York and Lancaster Regiment were held in reserve on the west bank between Talana Farm and Dawson's Corner (B22.c) noted:

> It soon became evident that there must be no promiscuous strolling about, as the enemy were apparently prepared to let go a salvo even on a party of three men, while farms and roads were well registered. Rifle batteries swept the road from Modder (400 metres west of Talana) and Talana to the canal, and were much used at night upon ration parties and reliefs, with considerable success.

The West Riding Division's tour of the Boesinghe trenches was described as one of 'comparative military inactivity', for it was neither in rest nor in action. This must have been reassuring to units like the Hallamshires

Men of the 27th German Infantry Regiment wearing the first respirators issued to them. The first British consignment of gas cylinders were despatched to France 10 July 1915.

in the forward trenches. On 13 July, a substantial bombardment of explosive and tear gas shells supported by rapid rifle fire punished the front line. The enemy massed in preparation for an attack but the artillery halted it. In two days within the alleged area of 'comparative military inactivity' the Hallamshires alone suffered one dead officer, two wounded and seventy-two other ranks dead or wounded.

Countless intelligence gathering patrols, deemed so important at the time, have faded into obscurity, overshadowed by clashes considered more significant. One such minor incident involved 8/West Yorkshires, who commenced a turn in the line on 13 July. A routine night patrol two nights later exemplified the courage and resourcefulness of the average infantry soldier. Lieutenant Wilkinson and Riflemen Mudd and Clough crossed No Man's Land and reached the enemy parapet. Unfortunately, Mudd was shot through the chest, and his cries of pain attracted hostile fire. While under fire, the officer and rifleman carried the wounded man back to the British line, but were unable to penetrate the wire. Rifleman Clough managed to negotiate the wire and set off for wire cutters, whilst Lieutenant Wilkinson remained with the wounded man. Clough returned with the cutters, and the party re-entered the line. Lieutenant Wilkinson received the Military Cross and Rifleman Clough received the Distinguished Conduct Medal for their cool and gallant action in this exploit. The next day, 3485 Rifleman F Mudd died; he is buried in New Irish Farm Cemetery, XVII E 8.

Lieutenant Anthony Slingsby, KinA on 16 July 1915.

Nearby, 1/6 Duke of Wellington had relieved 1/5 West Yorkshire in the front line between Turco Farm and Morteldje Estaminet on 13 July. They extended from E27 to E30. An enemy salient, known as Caesar's Nose, jutted into No Man's Land here; as a result, in E29 only twenty-five to thirty yards separated the adversaries. Snipers were particularly troublesome. On 16 July, as Lieutenant Anthony Slingsby was involved in laying a telephone wire in the trench opposite the enemy sap, he was killed. Captain Barclay Godfrey Buxton, 6/Duke of Wellington commented:

> They dropped a shell into our trench and we had a gap there, which I and another man filled up all night. There was a very real sense that they [Germans] were on top of us till we got the sandbags up. Then a wonderful fellow, Lieutenant Slingsby, the signal officer was

Private Stephen Bishop, who was killed by a grenade. He is commemorated on the Menin Gate.

killed laying a line across that gap. Anthony Slingsby was in charge of some boy scouts who won the Yorkshire Trophy, and he asked to join the battalion with his unit of boy scouts as the signalling section. He, possibly wrongly, always took the dangerous job, in case of his boys being hit. On that occasion, when he came up to lay the line, he got through the gap eleven yards from the Germans, and unfortunately got up too quick and was shot through the top of the head. When they got him down, we found underneath his hat, by his bed in battalion headquarters 'Mori Est Decorum Dulce', it is a glorious and dutiful thing to die for your country. He had obviously written it recently, we couldn't say whether he had written it that day, I don't think many had premonitions as clear as possibly that one did.

Despite the constant shelling and contrary to the modern general perception of staff officers the ageing divisional commander, Major-General Baldock, established his forward headquarters at Brielen in *Les Tres Tours* chateau. The General Staff Officers, 1st and 2nd Grade, the Brigade Major of the Royal Artillery and the Signal Company joined him. Allegedly, the general 'bade the band play at the chateau'… but such bold ventures were later abandoned. On the morning of 16 July, three salvoes slammed into the chateau and grounds. The following afternoon the shelling resumed and, unfortunately, the GOC, who was just crossing the bridge to the chateau, failed to reach cover in time. He sustained a severe head wound from which he eventually recovered but failed to regain command of a division he had led since 1911. His successor, General Edward Maxwell Percival CB DSO, had previously served with the Royal Artillery in the Burma, India and South Africa campaigns. He went to France in 1914, and had been acting as sub-Chief of Staff at General Headquarters. He would command the division until October 1917. The next day advanced

Les Tres Tours Chateau Brielen where Baldock was wounded while crossing the bridge

One of the many flimsy military bridges spanning the Yser canal.

headquarters moved approximately two miles to the rear, where they established themselves at Hospital Farm.

Life went on; as the staff departed, 6/West Yorkshires arrived at the chateau after a tour of the front line. They noted that the grounds were 'quite charming' and a wide moat full of fish surrounded the chateau. Their billets were holes in the ground, which successive battalions converted into shelters. During their six days held in reserve here, they managed a cricket match of the officers versus C Company; the other ranks won. Simple pleasures such as this took the troops' minds away from the horrors of trench warfare, but even out of the front line no one was safe.

When 7/West Yorkshire completed a tour of the front line just before midnight on 25 July they retired to dugouts in the west embankment of the canal. The enemy were all too aware considerable numbers of men were housed here and regularly shelled the bank. Throughout the 29th, from mid morning to midnight, 230 shells rained down on the embankment, collapsing a crowded dugout and damaging the bridge in three places. Second Lieutenant A R Glazebrook received the Military Cross for helping to dig out, at great personal risk, an officer and ten men from destroyed dugouts, thus saving nine lives. Lieutenant Richard Stanley Briggs died in the bunker and ten men were wounded.

In early August events to the south were to have their consequences on the northern part of the Salient. Due to the explosion of a mine at Hooge and the German use of flamethrowers, the 14th Division lost ground. On 9 August, the 6th Division counter attacked; they carried all their objectives, but suffered heavy casualties. The 49th Division were not involved in the attack yet deceived the opposition into believing that they were. As part of the ruse, bridges appeared across the canal, gaps were created in the wire, and artillery fired at intervals at the German front line. It was all smoke and mirrors, aimed to distract the enemy from the true objective. The resulting German barrage indicated that the sleight of hand had achieved the desired result, but claimed the inevitable casualties.

The Trenches

Throughout their occupancy of the sector, the troops toiled away improving their positions. Men in Brigade Reserve ate and slept by day and worked throughout the night. The British army initially did not name their front line trenches; instead, they divided the line into sections, identified by a letter and digits. This book covers the sections F35 to F30, E28 to E23 and D22 to D18. The extreme left section of British trench was F35 while D18 was slightly east of Turco Farm. However, communication trenches were named and are usually identifiable by the inclusion of lane, street or road in their title. Not surprisingly, the Yorkshire Territorials christened the local features and communication

Ladling mud out of the trenches.

trenches after places in their home county, hence Huddersfield Road (C.19.a.b), Skipton Road (C.13.c.d) and Knaresborough Castle (C.20.b.70.99) etc. Even so, sections such as D19 and D20 respectively became Willow Walk and Canadian Dugouts (C.14.d.15.c). Three light railways eased the burden of the carrying parties, whose loads were now pushed on trucks.

By mid-summer a decent trench system existed, communication trenches connected support and reserve lines and conditions were tolerable. Unfortunately, due to the danger, limited time and materials, insufficient means of draining the trenches were incorporated in their construction. The inadequacy of drains became apparent with the arrival of prolonged rain during August, when the trenches accumulated water. Another problem of trench warfare was the difficulty of manoeuvring a standard seven foot-nine inch stretcher around the trench traverses. Private William Edward Pinnington, 1/10 Liverpool Scottish, served as a stretcher bearer under the command of the battalion medical officer, Captain Noel Godfrey Chavasse. All too familiar with the problem of getting a stretcher along the trenches, Pinnington devised a short stretcher that allowed a wounded man to sit up, thereby reducing the need for a long stretcher. The 21 July 1915 trench trials of the four foot and five inches long stretcher satisfied the Divisional ADMS and the Divisional General, who both endorsed the fabrication of further stretchers and the design was patented on 3 August 1916. The simple canvas and wood invention probably saved many lives but arguably, had a folding stretcher been available to 1/4 Duke of Wellingtons, the battalion would not have lost an officer while rescuing a wounded man.

On 14 August, approximately three weeks after the first trials of Pinnington's stretcher, 1/4 Duke of Wellington's were in the Glimpse Cottage sector. As usual three companies held the front line, the fourth remained in reserve. Late in the afternoon, a dugout in A Company's part of the line was blown in, burying a number of men. Despite heavy artillery and small arms fire, Captain M P Andrews dashed to the wreckage and six men were extricated, of whom three were already dead. One was so seriously wounded that he required urgent medical attention, but the trenches were too narrow for a stretcher case. The only option was to carry him across the open ground. Captain Andrews climbed out the trench and helped to lift the wounded man before setting off with the stretcher-

Captain M P Andrews.

69

bearers across the bullet swept open ground. Before the group could reach the safety of a communication trench, the officer was hit in the head, he died almost at once. He is buried in Colne Valley Cemetery, C.7.

On 1 June the 6th Division had taken over the front line extending from the Ypres-Roulers railway to Wieltje. The 49th Division's frontage further shrank on 24 August, when the 1/Kings Shropshire Light Infantry (KSLI) of 16 Brigade in the 6th Division took over the Turco Farm and Morteldje Estaminet front. This arranged encroachment by the 6th Division allowed the 49th Division front to be held by two instead of three brigades, the third brigade then being allowed a twelve day rest. Theoretically, each battalion spent roughly eleven days in support, eleven days in reserve and the same in the front line. The rest periods were generally spent in Coppernolle Wood.

But there was no rest in the Salient front line on 25 September 1915, the opening day of the Battle of Loos. The 6th Division was ordered to the south to attack and capture Bellewaarde Farm in an attempt to draw the enemy's reserves northwards, or at least to hold German troops in the sector. At 4.30 am, near Turco Farm, the artillery was to blow gaps in the enemy wire opposite the 1/4 Duke of Wellingtons. Thousands of phosphorus smoke bombs were thrown from the front line trenches, covering No Man's Land in an impenetrable mist. The intention was to make the Germans evacuate their front line, allowing 1/4 Duke of Wellingtons to advance and capture the deserted trenches. Expecting an imminent attack, the enemy response was immediate, artillery strafed the front line and communication trenches, supported by heavy rifle and machine-gun fire. Sentries of 6/West Yorkshires reported seeing the enemy stand up on his firestep and pour rapid fire into the mist. As the smoke cleared, snipers picked off the freely moving Germans, who were preparing to repel an attack. In the face of such resistance, however, no attack was launched and by 7.30 am the guns of both sides had practically ceased firing.

Once darkness descended upon the battlefield, the troops not assigned duties took advantage of the lull in hostilities. Some may have written letters home, while junior officers wrote letters to the next of kin of men who had made the supreme sacrifice that day or compiled the entries on Army Form C2118, commonly known as the War Diary or Intelligence Summary.

Battalion War Diaries do not generally provide an objective account of their men in the front line but often remain an invaluable insight into the conditions and activities experienced by them. 6/West Yorkshires' entry for 4 October 1915 is typical.

Enemy bombarded our left company with hand bombs and large

German machine gun crew grimace for the camera.

trench mortars, 'Rum Jars', Bombs fell in our trenches, 'Rum Jars' behind. We replied energetically with hand bombs, and got retaliation from our artillery, 12.20 am. Bombing attack on left company begun by enemy. We replied with two bombs to every German one, until he gave up. Probably enemy bombing attacks were to cover working parties. Enemy doing a lot of wiring in front of his line, noise of driving of stakes fairly continuous, 12 noon. Enemy put heavy and light trench mortars into F31. We replied with rifle grenades and trench howitzer bombs, silencing him effectively. Enemy shelled our Companies in F31 and F32 with high explosives. Enemy seen ladling water out of his trenches. Heavy rain. Trenches collapsing in many places.

Further south, High Command Redoubt overlooked the British lines from where the Germans appeared to have dispensed death with relative immunity. *The History of the 6/West Yorkshire Regiment* records:

D19, D20, Willow Walk and Canadian Dugouts became quickly notorious for various forms of acute unpleasantness. The whole of this section of the line is over looked by what was known as High Command, though the name appears on no official maps. The High

Command was a slight rise in the ground (29 metre contour) *which had been strongly fortified by the enemy, and was about 250 yards from our front line near Willow Walk.*

In keeping with the British frontline rotational system, on 7 October 1/4 King's Own Yorkshire Light Infantry (KOYLI) relieved 5/KOYLI in the front line of the La Belle Alliance sector. The incoming troops took up positions in D21 and D22, where they received the usual bombardments. High Command became a favourite haunt of snipers, who from their dry vantage point picked off the British as they scurried from post to post. On the night of the 10th a searchlight, situated in the redoubt, probed D20, as a trolley mounted machine-gun opened fire on the barricaded front. The next day a German balloon soared into the sky, directing some fifty shells onto the British lines. Little damage was done to the trenches, but two men died and another was wounded. The next night Lieutenant J H Bates and a strong patrol ventured out in front of D21 to investigate mounds believed to be old dug outs. They returned and reported them to be an old S shaped trench containing eight dead French soldiers in full marching order; and many others were lying about. At 6.30 am the Germans used howitzers, field guns and trench mortars to bombard the communication trench to D22 and the ground between the front and support trenches. 1/4 KOYLI replied with trench mortars and the situation quietened down after British howitzers bombarded the High Redoubt Fort (also referred to as High Command).

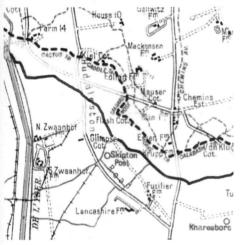

After seventy-five minutes the hostile bombardment faded away, allowing the British an opportunity to access the damage. The British parapets and communication trench were slightly damaged, a West Bomb Throwing machine was badly damaged (possibly to the relief of the men ordered to use the infernal invention) and ten yards of communication trench between 49th and 6th Divisions was 'blown down'. The war diary does not record any 1/4 KOYLI casualties. During the night a German patrol in No Man's Land left a calling card in the form of a flag, this had a blue background with white crossings and a star. During the next day (13 October) German shelling wounded four men.

A trench map showing the German salient Caesar's Nose.

Looking from the British position toward the cemetery sited on Caesar's Nose.

After darkness fell the battalion proceeded to Elverdinghe, where the battalion took over billets vacated by 5/KOYLI, who then returned to front line duties.

After a six-day respite, on 14 October, the 1/4 Duke of Wellingtons relieved the 1/5 West Yorkshire Regiment in the Glimpse Cottage region. To the right were C Company, in the centre A Company, with D Company on their left, B Company remained in support. Facing the frontage of C Company was the salient known as Caesar's Nose, from which an old communication trench ran across No Man's Land, a legacy from a period when the opposing front lines were part of the same network. Each side created a bombing block within this bitterly contested feature which, due to the undulating ground, could not be protected by rifle fire. Instead, machine-gunners swept the ground around the trench, aided by two-inch trench mortars and a group of battalion bombers who remained at the saphead.

At 1.30 pm on 16 October a severe trench mortar and artillery barrage rained down upon the sector as far back as battalion headquarters. In anticipation of an attack upon the saphead and its associated trench some thirty yards to the rear, 'Stand To' was ordered and two platoons carried bombs and ammunition forward whilst reinforcements were despatched to the sap head, the focus of the enemy's attention. This was the first occasion the battalion experienced a prolonged bombardment and for three hours, in compliance with orders, they held their fire. The majority of shells were falling behind the front line. Nevertheless, there were sufficient 'on target' to inflict casualties, especially among the flanking companies. At 4.30 pm a group of Germans rose from their trench and proceeded to cut an opening through their wire, close to the saphead. The men of A Company had patiently waited for three hours for such an opportunity and, ignoring the bursting shells, mounted the firestep and

73

Boesinghe Chateau.

exacted their revenge upon the working party.

Meanwhile a shell destroyed the bombing block and covered the garrison in debris. After extricating themselves, the men created a new bombing block just in time to repel a fresh attack. A score of German bombers had crawled over the folds in the terrain and commenced bombing the saphead. Most of the stick grenades fell short, unlike the grenades of the British bombers. Throughout the shelling four hostile attacks were launched but all were dispersed by bomb and machine-gun fire. Around 6.00 pm the Germans realised the futility of their attacks and the shelling gradually reduced in tempo.

The saphead and sections of the line were severely damaged but the enemy had been denied their objective. The casualties sustained on 16 October were Second Lieutenant Ernest Taylor, who died of wounds (Hospital Farm Cemetery, E.9) and twelve other ranks. The losses were not significant but it should be remembered that this was the battalion's first heavy encounter with the enemy.

'Our chief enemy out here is mud, and the Bosche make a bad second!'

Even in fine weather, the trenches near Boesinghe had the reputation of being the 'worst on the divisional front' due to the proximity of the enemy and the commanding position of their lines. The onset of autumn brought bouts of heavy rain that drained off Pilckem Ridge into the low-lying trenches. On 30 October, 1/4 Duke of Wellingtons commenced their first tour of duty on the extreme left of the line, which consisted mainly of

74

sandbag breastworks. The battalion historian noted that,

> The front line was in places more than two feet deep in semi-liquid mud and parts of it were entirely isolated from neighbouring posts, except by cross-country routes; stretches of the communication trenches were waist deep in water. And this was the result of only about two days of steady rain! For the next two months conditions gradually became worse...

Soup kitchens and hot food were on offer to front line troops but seldom reached the front line. In mud where it took an hour for a man to move one hundred yards, few considered the effort expended in a journey to reserve positions for hot sustenance safe or worthwhile. The infantrymen were required to spend long periods standing in the putrid water lining the trenches and became susceptible to a condition known as trench feet, a fungal infection of the feet. Prolonged exposure to the cold and wet could turn the foot gangrenous and lead to amputation. The division made great efforts to minimise the effects of trench foot, aided by the arrival of thousands of tins of anti-frostbite grease provided by the York Territorial Association. Thousands of thigh high gumboots arrived and each man entering the line took several pairs of clean socks, though how they managed to change them while in a quagmire is not recorded. On relief, the outgoing battalion took off their boots at Essex Farm, and laid them out for the incoming battalion. In darkness and in fields ankle deep in mud, the incoming soldiers struggled to find a matching pair of footwear. However, as a result of the preventative measures introduced within the division, total 'trench foot' cases were an acceptable 760 cases, which averaged out at six men a day. (The mathematics indicate that the figures equate to a four month period).

British humour prevailed over flooded trenches.

A welcome escape from the miserable existence in the line was periods spent in Divisional Reserve. Over three miles west of Boesinghe sprawled a network of army camps located in the Coppernollehoek area.

At the camps baths and clean cloths were provided, a little training was attempted but demands for working parties constantly interrupted proceedings. After 146 Brigade completed a seventeen-day stint in one of the camps, 6/West Yorkshire returned to the Turco Farm area on 2 November. The outgoing 148 Brigade had conducted a great deal of work in the line. Second Line trenches at Vicar's Lane had been improved and new dugouts and living-in trenches constructed, such as Dawson's City (C.14.d.2.0.b), named after the commander of 148 Brigade. Unfortunately, shells and rain destroyed their work and when 146 Brigade took over the sector the conditions were at the limit of a man's endurance. A quagmire of mud reached back to the road where the Battalion Transport lines stood. The horse lines were some distance from the road and a knee-deep morass of mud separated the transport and horse lines. The quagmire sapped the horses' strength and none were strong enough to pull a cart into the wagon lines, so all food, man and equine, was transported by pack horse from the Quartermaster's stores.

The *History of the 1/6 West Yorkshire Regiment* includes an extract of a letter sent home by Private 2190 E M Kermode, a member of the original battalion.

> 'You may think I am in the trenches. Disabuse yourself of that idea at once. We are inhabiting canals which are of four varieties. 1. Full of water. 2. Full of mud. 3. Full of earth. 4. Drains. The ones full of water are easiest to move in, but rather disappointing as places of habitation. We sit on the firing step all night, and wheeze and spit and smoke. Cigarettes save the situation. Fires are impossible: sleep impossible. To keep warm is only possible occasionally – to keep dry a farce. It rained for four days and filled up the trenches – canals I mean – and then it stopped and froze. Trench feet and frost-bite claimed five of our section of nine. When I tell you that we walk across the top in daylight, you will see that we cared nothing for our lives at that time. No one uses the trenches at night, they are too dangerous. One might be suffocated or drowned...
> [Sergeant Edward M Kermode received a DCM (LG 15 March 1916) for his actions during the 19 December gas attack. He later gained a commission and subsequently won a DSO, MC and Bar.]

Water also accumulated in the opposition's trenches, but their pumps ejected the water onto No Man's Land which, due to the incline, inevitably drained into the British trenches. The prolonged rainfall caused devastation within the trench system. In mid November, Halifax Road communication trench collapsed. Throughout the sector, hundreds of yards of trenches suffered the same fate, forcing the evacuation of long sections of the front line. A series of isolated posts, spaced fifty-yards

The shelled wood of Boesinghe Chateau. Notice the four military grave markers.

apart, were the only means of holding the front. The posts were usually three feet deep in water and the only means of accessing them was across open ground, suicidal by day and extremely hazardous by night. During daylight, enemy snipers made the most of the opportunities presented by the conditions of the trenches. As no movement was possible during daytime, the wounded had to remain in the line until darkness descended; the journey to the canal bank could take stretcher-bearers two or three hours. The task was fraught with danger, for machine-guns swept the open ground on the off-chance of hitting a patrol. There were a few instances in the division where men drowned in communication trenches. Nonetheless, the vulnerability of the abandoned areas resulted in a significant increase in defensive work, for at night the enemy could easily enter the isolated posts. A policy of 'live and let live' set in, which was just as well, for rifles were normally clogged with mud. It proved impossible to keep rifles clean and any attack would need to be dealt with by bayonet. Troops in reserve worked to improve the drains or attempted to clear the mud and water from the communication trenches.

The conditions were so detrimental to health that front line garrisons were in place for only forty-eight hours, later reduced by half. During this period a man experienced biting cold and would be completely saturated; if the suction of the mud had not claimed his gumboots, they would be full of water. Added to this were tiredness, physical pain and the stress of not knowing if you would complete the duty. As an example, consider the result of the 1/4 Duke of Wellington's forty-eight hour stretch in the

line. An officer and twenty-four men held the post; at the end of the tour, the officer brought out a signaller and three other ranks and all the others were casualties.

Amid the lunarscape of holes and desolation, daily survival took precedence over fighting the enemy. The sternest test of all for infantry is to hold a line while under constant bombardment from artillery. The incessant shelling claimed many lives but, with indominatable spirit, the hard-pressed infantry strove to hold the line and rescue as many of their injured comrades as possible. The *History of the 1/4 Duke of Wellington's Regiment* admirably sums up the situation:

> *The soldier in battle has excitement, and a good deal of exhilaration, to help him through; but the Yorkshiremen who faced the enemy near Boesinghe in 1915 had neither of these. Theirs was*

heroism of a far higher order – the heroism which, with no excitement to buoy them up, can make men coolly and quietly face horror and death in their worst forms.

On 6 November, a trench being blown in, stretcher-bearers were prevented from rescuing two wounded men. Without any thought for his own safety, 2503 Private A Dodd went to their rescue under very heavy shell and trench mortar fire. After dressing their wounds and bringing them safely back, he returned and extricated a partly buried man, only to find he had died. On the same day, near Turco Farm, an exploding shell buried four other men. In full view of the enemy fire trench and despite being shelled by a high velocity quick-firing gun, 559 Sergeant A L Pearson, 1983 Corporal E Green and 2634 Private A Benson, displaying equal valour and devotion, successfully rescued the four men.

Two days later one of the battalion sergeants had his leg crushed by the blowing in of a dugout and Captain H J Burke, attached to the regiment from the Royal Army Medical Corps, found that an immediate amputation was necessary. In order to save time, he fearlessly crawled across open ground to get his equipment. The enemy turned a machine-gun on him but, in spite of their fire, he returned the same way. Inside the trench, in the middle of a substantial bombardment, assisted by Lieutenant Campbell K Alexander, who had no medical knowledge, Burke coolly amputated the crushed limb. For his superb act of courage, Burke received the Military Cross.

Second Lieutenant Alexander, on 11 November, while at Hale Farm, gallantly helped to dig out two men who had been buried while the enemy shelled the position with their howitzers. In the rescue he was assisted by 2229 Private W Steed, whose reward was the DCM.

To men hardened in battle, who had witnessed death in all its macabre variations, the haunting fear of being buried alive must have been prominent in their thoughts.

Sergeant Samuel Meekosha VC.

One such rescue on 19 November resulted in the first award of the Victoria Cross (gazetted January 1916) to the 49th Division, to Corporal Samuel Meekosha of B Company, 1/6 West Yorkshire Regiment. The Bradford territorial soldier was born in Leeds on 16 September 1893. The unusual surname came from his Russian Polish father, though he had an Irish mother.

Corporal Meekosha was with a platoon of about twenty non commissioned officers and men who were holding an isolated trench (the Pump Room). During a very heavy bombardment by the enemy, six of the platoon were killed and seven wounded, while all the remainder were more or less buried. When the senior NCOs had been either killed or wounded, Corporal Meekosha at once took command. He sent a runner for assistance and, in

Gallantry award recipients pose for the camera: Pte E. J. Wilkinson; L/Cpl E. Johnson; Cpl J Sayers; Sgt S. Meekosha VC. Promotions probably followed after the incident.

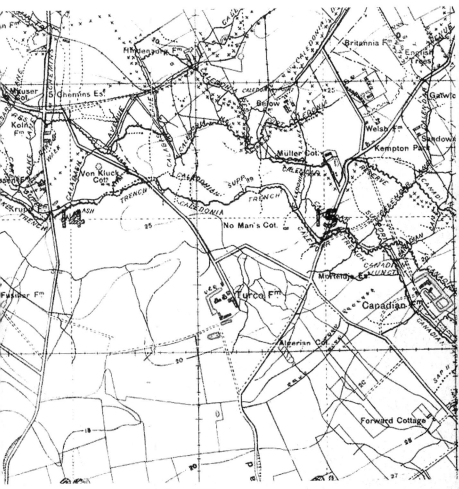

Trench map corrected to June 1917.

spite of no less than ten more big shells falling within twenty yards of him, continued to dig out the wounded and buried men in full view of the enemy and at close range from the German trenches. By his promptitude and magnificent courage and determination, he saved at least four lives.

The Battalion history claims that three NCOs were awarded the DCM, the recipients were Privates 1266 E J Wilkinson, 3225 E Johnson and 2626 Private J Sayers, also gazetted on 22 January 1916. Due to his unusual surname a reserved Meekosha VC disliked the fame and public attention the award attracted. He was so uncomfortable with this that in 1941 he changed his name by deed poll to Ingham (taken from his mother's maiden name Cunningham). He died in December 1950.

The attack of 19 December 1915

After the April gas attack Allied troops were issued with rudimentary gas masks. Improved designs followed and in late 1915 troops were issued with a material hood soaked in chemical for protection against chlorine gas. The P helmet had an easily broken single mica window and lacked an outlet valve, which made breathing laboured. Scientists soon developed an improved version, having two glass eyepieces and an outlet valve and capable of filtering out phosgene and chlorine gas. Each front line soldier received the new PH helmet but, due to insufficient availability, retained the P helmet as a reserve.

Intelligence had reached the staff of Second Army, through captured prisoners, of an impending gas attack in the Salient on the scale of the spring gas attack. The allied armies were now much better prepared to counter such a development. At night, patrols were very active searching for any signs of gas cylinders in the enemy lines. One patrol reported a hammering and a great deal of coughing on the eve of the attack. Sergeant B M Riley, of A Company 1/6 West Yorkshire, on hearing of gas cylinders in the enemy front and reading of the Kaiser's visit to Belgium on 19 December, predicted an attack between 4.00 am and daylight that day; a prophecy which came true.

Two days before the attack, on 17 December, enemy shelling was unusually heavy and in many places what was left of the front line trench

With the wind in the right direction – gas blowing towards Allied lines.

became merely a row of shell holes. The next day the enemy hardly fired a shell and the silence seemed ominous. British artillery had become more plentiful, and it now attempted to damage the German trenches at points where attack troops might gather and also destroy any gas cylinders in place. Throughout Saturday, the wind blew steadily from the east northeast, but at sunset it dropped to a light breeze.

A misty dawn broke on 19 December and sentries reported hissing noises and a white vapour rising in No Man's Land. 1/4 KOYLI were located in the line E27, 28 and 29, and the War Diary records.

A soldier wearing a PH helmet. The hoods were tucked inside the neck of the jacket to provide a seal against the gas.

> *4.50 am. A hissing noise like a fast running motor car was heard in the German lines. Very shortly after, the presence of cylinder gas, said to be Phosgene, was detected in the air. Warning was given, tube helmets put on and rapid fire opened on the enemy's parapet with rifles and machine guns. 'SOS Gas' was sent to the artillery, who immediately opened fire. No infantry attack was made but later a German patrol, numbering about ten men, was seen advancing towards our trenches. Rifle fire was opened on them and they dispersed, only one man being seen to regain the German trench. The enemy heavily bombarded our front line throughout the day.*

Around 5.45 am the enemy bombarded the lines from the canal bank near Boesinghe as far south as Wieltje. A heavy bombardment of shells of every calibre descended upon the canal bank, communication trenches and reserve positions. The deadly fumes reached the support trenches and crowded dugouts, where sleeping men were gassed before they could be roused. Only one bridge remained useable and telephone lines were severed. Gongs and horns sounded the alarm, calling men to their battle stations. At 6.30 am companies in reserve received the orders to move up into defence positions, all companies taking the most direct routes. The gas shells exploded with 'a dull splash' and their almost silent arrival gassed men before they recognised the danger. They lay on the ground contorted with agony, foaming at the mouth and fighting for air. An almost blinded man wrote from his hospital bed:

> *...The whiz bangs were awful, and an enfilade machine gun fire*

A well trod path alongside the Yperlee which ran parallel with the canal until flowing into it, to the rear of sector F34. Dugouts were cut into the banking.

swept the top of the trench, so they (the wounded) had to be dragged along the mud, using their hands. All leg and body wounds. There they lay all day...

Fresh cylinder gas discharges occurred at twenty minutes intervals throughout the hour long artillery bombardment. The expected attack failed to materialise, due to the French and British artillery pulverising the German parapets and the prolonged rapid fire of infantrymen. Small parties of Germans rose from their trenches but, in the face of withering rifle and artillery fire, their advance melted away. By 7 am quiet had descended upon the 49th Division front (further north the French suffered another gas attack at 9 am) until early afternoon, when intermittent shelling began, lasting until the early hours of the next morning. A Royal Artillery Officer wrote

... It was the most awful yet magnificent sight I have ever seen. The whole country was shaking with the explosion of shells, mostly big; and a church near my headquarters was hit with a seventeen-inch shell and blown to bits. The sky was one great glow like a vast electric light, and the atmosphere was laden with a choking and sickly heaviness...

Gas still lingered in sections of the trenches throughout the day and even the next night. The ground over which the cloud passed was covered with powdered crystals like hoar frost. Investigations showed that, if disturbed by feet, the crystals gave off a quantity of gas so great that gas hoods were required. Some authorities say that it was the strongest concentration of phosgene cylinder gas sent over by the enemy during the war; Canadians on parade at Bailleul, twelve miles to the rear, felt the effects.

The West Riding Territorials casualties for 19 December were four officers and forty-six other ranks killed. The wounded comprised two officers and 106 other ranks, whilst eight officers and 191 other ranks were gassed. The importance of their actions cannot be underestimated for, in the words of the GOC of VI Corps, 'the coolness of the troops saved the Army from disaster'.

The Monmouth Pioneers

Faced with constant maintenance and expansion of the network of trenches, the army established pioneer battalions. The military recognised that battalions raised from mining areas were adept with shovel and pick and possessed the necessary knowledge to construct light railways, fire steps and dig a labyrinth of trenches. In early September, the 3/Monmouthshire Regiment was assigned to 49th Division as pioneers. Battalion headquarters and billets were established in the grounds of Elverdinghe Chateau. Two companies of Monmouthshire pioneers established forward billets at Dunbarton Dugouts, in the west embankment. Hazardous nights at the front were passed in the backbreaking excavation of drainage ditches, whilst every six days they rotated with the companies within the chateau grounds.

Little of note occurred until 5.30 am on 19 December when, due to the gas attack, the Monmouths' Elverdinghe attachment was ordered to the canal bank. Three hours later the canal bank attachment was manning the reserve fire trenches and the Elverdinghe attachment occupied dugouts on the canal bank. One machine gun team covered the Elverdinghe to Boesinghe road while another was set up on Mill Mound in Elverdinghe. The expected attack never materialised in full, but the infantry crammed into the trenches were subjected to shelling and gas. Among the heroes of the hour was 1425 Lance Corporal Dixon, whose DCM citation states: *He volunteered with a comrade* (1317 Private G Powell, who received the MM) *to cross a canal and bring in two men who were believed to be incapacitated. They succeeded, under fire, in bringing in one man, badly gassed.*

The rescued man may have been one of three who died of wounds, two more were killed, and three dozen more are listed as casualties.

Despite the hostilities the combatants thoughts probably focussed on the approaching Christmas period, an alleged time of peace and goodwill to all men. The previous year both sides had observed a Christmas truce and the Germans tentatively sought another truce. On Christmas Day, on the extreme left of the British line, the Germans in *Fortin* 17 erected a Christmas tree. They called out to members of 1/5 Duke of Wellingtons, 'Don't shoot and we won't', but recalling the attack a few days previously, the British fired. Two days after Christmas the Monmouthshire pioneers were relieved in readiness for a move to the Somme. At 2.30 pm on 27 December the battalion paraded in the grounds of Elverdinghe Chateau, prior to moving out. An ominous sound was heard, like an oncoming train, and a seventeen inch shell launched from a naval gun in Houthulst Forest exploded in their midst. In the blink of an eye, thirty-nine men died (*Soldiers Died* gives forty-three deaths) and thirty-three more were wounded.

During the final days of 1915 the division prepared for a move to Calais, where they remained until February, when the revitalised division moved to the Somme.

"If I were to pick from a variegated career the period when physical wretchedness reached its stark bottom, I should choose the last five months at Ypres in 1915. We started in exuberant health and spirits. At Christmas, those who were left crawled out, broken in body and almost heart, staggering and falling like drunken men after a march of five miles. Rain fell incessantly."

Sergeant J E Yates, 6/West Yorkshire

Chapter Five

IT'S GRIM UP NORTH

As the Yorkshire territorial battalions filed out of the line, the 14th (Light) Division took over the front, extending from Irish Farm (near St Jean) to the extreme left of the line. After a week, the line shifted to the right when 43 Brigade took over 16 Brigade's part of 6th Division's sector. This caused some resentment, for the previous month the 14th Division had fronted the sector unaided.

As the energy sapping wet weather continued, the War Diarist of 6/Somerset Light Infantry (LSLI) recorded that the three platoons entering the front line in D21 and D22 on 4/5 January took over 'thigh gum boots in a very wet condition'. No line existed, merely isolated posts, as the lines were still full of water and falling to pieces. Conditions for the four platoons holding Spahi Farm and Dawson City were much better

West Riding Territorials looking more like brigands than soldiers.

off, as they had good Royal Engineer dugouts; the remaining platoons were in rest billets in farms around Elverdinghe. Conditions in the forward trenches continued to give cause for concern and as a result troops in the front line were relieved every forty-eight hours to prevent sickness.

The almost impossible conditions prevented the improvement of the trenches, but each night working parties strove to develop the defences and increase the height of the barbed wire defences. On the night of the 8th, while on such a working party, four men of 6/Somersets were killed and four wounded. Little of great note appears to have occurred during January. However, 14th Division headquarters appear to have expected an attack for, on 26 January 1916, brigade officers were ordered to prepare defensive schemes. A directive marked 'Secret', issued to 43 Brigade, contains a paragraph advising:

...The present conditions of the trenches renders the task of defending the line more difficult than would be the case if the fire and support trenches, splinter proof accommodation for troops etc, were in good condition. This must not, however, be allowed to affect the usual principle of defence. If attacked, the front line must be held as long as possible by the troops and machine-guns detailed for its defence. This order cannot be too strongly impressed on all concerned. Supporting troops must always be kept in such trenches as can be maintained, ready to counter attack if the front line is lost. Machine-guns must be disposed to the rear of the front line, ready to assist such counter attacks. It is more than ever necessary that all defences should be strongly wired and well defended by machine-guns, which can play such an important part in defence. All trenches in front of the X Line will be considered as the front line.

In compliance with the above order, the front line battalions intensified their efforts to create impenetrable swathes of barbed wire. Wiring parties were an established nocturnal occupation, for scarcely a dark night passed without wiring parties furtively entering No Man's Land to improve or repair the wire damaged by shell fire. On the night of 1st February, two Germans were mistaken for British as they worked away in a sixty-yard gap between two British wiring parties. The clandestine wire cutters were opening up a passage through the wire in readiness for an attack. Despite disguising their handiwork, the breaks became apparent upon close examination. Between 9.00 am and 9.45 am (recorded times vary) on 2 February, German artillery and trench mortars opened fire on D.19, 20 and 21, continuing until 11.26 am. When the guns ceased, the enemy came out through saps cut under their parapets and advanced on the British trenches from three directions. The first small party advanced

Germany infantry pose for a Pilckem postcard, sent home by *Feldpost* in March 1916.

from near C.15.c.9.8 (near Morteldje Estaminet), while another came from the direction of No Man's Cottage. Second Lieutenant Paris (10/Durham LI), who was observing from D20, reported four small parties of seven advancing on D21 and left of D20, whilst a dozen strong group came from Duck's Bill. An estimated 120 men advanced from opposite D21 in support of this advance. The Germans were lightly equipped and had fixed bayonets and either ran or crawled through the long grass covering No Man's Land.

The SOS was sent up as British rifles opened up on the advanced parties who had reached the wire. Lieutenant G Wood, previously completely buried by a shell, emerged to direct calmly the repulse of the Germans near his wire (he received the MC). In reply to Paris's urgent signal, shells from B Battery of 47 Brigade devastated the largest group. The French on the left also co-operated and British heavies opened fire on the German position known as High Command (C.14.b.15.a) and their front and second lines. As soon as the barrage began, the majority of the Germans immediately returned to their trenches: some reached the dugouts at C.14.d.3.9 and 5.9, while others took cover in shell holes. A few men were shot twenty to thirty yards in front of the wire, while at C.14.d.7.7 (near Turco Farm) small arms fire killed two Germans who had almost reached the front post. Sergeant Warren 'had excellent sport' throughout the day shooting at Germans crawling in the long grass.

During the repulse, the Durhams incurred ten other rank casualties, five were killed by shells and one by bullet, two were wounded and two shell shocked.

This was the last significant incident in this theatre for the division, which received orders on 7 February to prepare for a divisional relief by the 20th (Light) Division. Over several nights the incoming division gradually exchanged positions with the outgoing troops. Two brigades would hold the front line in positions numbered B15-17, D19-22 and E23 in the right brigade sector. The left brigade was responsible for E24-29 and F30-35. Inadvertently, the planned relief occurred when the enemy launched a series of minor assaults within the Salient. These attacks aimed to secure local vantage points and distract attention away from the

Scene of the German attacks launched during February 1916.

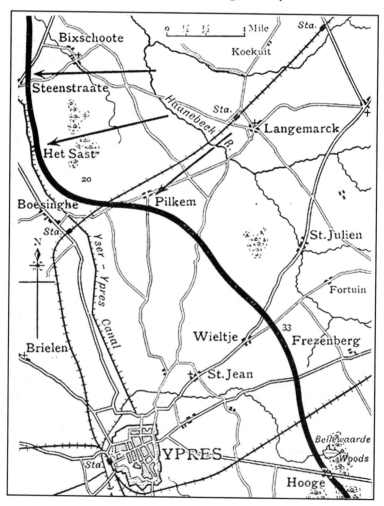

operations near Verdun, scheduled to commence on 21 February. In the extreme north of the Salient, where British troops linked with Joffre's army, after several days of 'softening up' shelling upon Steenstratt, Het Sas and Pilckem, the German IV Corps attacked on 12 February.

At 9.30 pm on 11 February 12/Rifle Brigade (20th Division) detrained at Goldfish Chateau, north of Ypres. The battalion moved off, and passed through Brielen during a bombardment of 77 mm shells and arrived ninety minutes later at Dawson's Corner. Guides then led the battalion to their canal bank and front line positions on the far left of the British line. At midnight, 12/Rifle Brigade commenced the relief of 9/Kings Royal Rifle Corps (KRRC), 42 Brigade, in the isolated stretches of E28 to F35 (part of F32 and all of F33 to F35 are now beneath an industrial park). The trenches were all in a bad state of repair and the parapets were very low and poor. No communication trenches existed and it was almost impossible to reach these very wet places by day.

The War Diary of 12/Rifle Brigade notes that at 2.00 am, while the relief was still in progress, a bomb attack was made on trenches F34 and F35, whilst considerable artillery and trench mortar fire fell on Wellgate and Wyatts Lane. A three-pronged attack on F34 was repulsed by rifle and grenades, killing five Germans. Meanwhile, on the right, a party of German bombers came along the parapet of a disused trench and jumped into part of F35, held by a bombing section and six men. A Rifle Brigade sergeant shot one German, whilst another wounded by a grenade surrendered; the remainder slipped away. Due to the darkness, the numbers involved were not clear, but the wounded prisoner reported that a German sergeant major and forty men had attacked F35. Simultaneous to this attack, the Germans attacked the head of the sap at F35. The British grenades soon ran out and the enemy were able to bomb their way along the entire length of F35.

Due to the destruction of the Fargate bomb store the previous night, insufficient bombs were available and it proved very difficult in getting bombs forward, as the trenches were knee deep in mud. In response to a request for assistance, two 12/KRRC bombing sections arrived. Supported by these two sections, Second Lieutenant Gribble, (12/Rifle Brigade) counter attacked and thirty-minutes later re-captured F35 and a few yards of German trench.

The Germans now withdrew beyond bombing range and bombarded the trench with trench mortars and artillery, forcing the British to withdraw as the trench became blown in. The German artillery slackened at daybreak. During the morning, the battalion was reinforced by three 12/KRRC bombing sections, three bombing sections from 6/KSLI and two 12/KRRC platoons. At 2.30 pm, the German artillery fire increased

Another example of a military footbridge spanning the canal.

considerably upon the front line and canal banks. Another attack seemed inevitable, so two companies of 6/KSLI moved up in support.

At 4.30 pm the German artillery lifted and fired barrages on the canal banks and roads behind the canal, whilst three infantry attacks were made on F34, F30 and E28. They failed to enter F34, due to steady rifle and grenade fire. At F30, a slightly wounded Second Lieutenant F J Fish, who commanded a thirty strong garrison, now reduced to a sergeant and seven men, beat back the attack. Within the almost destroyed E28, the men commanded by Second Lieutenant F Lockwood-Wingate retained all the remaining bays and repelled the attack. About 6.00 pm, when darkness descended, the gunfire ceased.

When the bombardment began Captain K R Habershon left battalion headquarters (C.13.a.2.4.), sited near Bridge 6D, and headed for the front line. The five bridges across the canal were under German fire and only 6D was practicable for daylight use. As the firing on Bridge 6D was very intense he took shelter in a dugout, where he died when a shell destroyed his shelter. By 6.30 pm the German artillery fire had practically ceased. At night reinforcements arrived at the forward positions and work continued all night repairing and clearing the trenches. 12/Rifle Brigade casualties for the night of 11/ 12 February comprised one officer killed and three wounded; twenty-two other ranks killed, eighty-eight wounded and thirty-nine missing. 12/Rifle Brigade War Diary noted:

The west bank of canal and bridges was very heavily shelled by 5.9 and 8 inch howitzers. It was computed that 300 enemy guns were firing on the battalion front. During the bombardment, all front line trenches were severely damaged. E29 was obliterated, E28 was practically destroyed with the exception of three bays, F30 was also severely damaged.

To the right of 12/Rifle Brigade the incoming 6/Kings Shropshire Light Infantry relieved their brother battalion, 5/KSLI of 14th Division, in the line between E24 to E28. These positions extended from approximately forward of Glimpse Cottage to the front facing Lancashire Farm. Other companies occupied the support trenches and canal bank. As the riflemen on their left were repulsing the Germans, attempts were made to seize a trench still occupied by 5/KSLI, but they were driven away. During the bombardment, four officers died and a collapsed hut injured another. Among the other ranks, nineteen were killed and three mortally wounded, whilst a further forty-six received wounds.

The French and the left of the British lines also received the full brunt of the bombardment, while other parts received less attention. At 2.00 pm on 12 February, 10/Durham LI in the line opposite High Command suffered an erratic bombardment. During the shelling, parties of the enemy advanced from High Command but turned back in the face of British shelling. Heavy and light mortars targeted the British trenches for several hours and at one stage as many as five bombs were visible in the

Belgian trench mortar bombers at Boesinghe, 1916.

A German sniper (from an
August 1915 edition of
L'Illustration)

air at once. The mortars appeared to be mounted on a tramway behind the enemy lines, making them extremely difficult to pinpoint and eliminate. During the onslaught, Regimental Sergeant Major A Noble was killed while crawling over open ground, leading some men to their post. The howitzers wiped out the machine-gun detachment and destroyed all dugouts. Second Lieutenant Ord Bell did excellent work in the demolished D21 by moving men from position to position and keeping their spirits up. The bombardment gradually abated but not before inflicting on the battalion eight dead, twelve wounded and one man gassed. In the early hours of a clear and frosty morning, 11/Rifle Brigade (20th Division) relieved 10/Durhams.

After serving nine months in the Salient, 14th Division departed on 21 February.

The onset of spring did little to improve the conditions. For example, the War Diarist of 7/Somerset LI, holding the line between Lancashire Farm and the bombing post Grouse Butts, complained:

The trenches were waterlogged and there was no dugouts of any description for officers or men. Only company headquarters had a certain amount of shelter, the rest had to 'stick it', sitting on the fire-steps up to their knees in water when they were resting. Private B Wright was one of those stuck in this godforsaken spot until a shell released him from his misery, on 25 February 1916 [they buried him in Essex Farm I D 19].

Within the Salient shells fell with the monotony of a dripping tap, and their casualties were supplemented by snipers who had honed their deadly art to perfection. Second Lieutenant R A M Lutener had trained the snipers of the 6/KSLI to an excellent standard. Their proficiency drew the attention of the Corps Commander, Lord Cavan, who ordered the other units in his command to work along similar lines. On 6 April an enemy sniper claimed three victims. As one of Lutener's best marksmen had failed to eliminate the sharpshooter concealed in No Man's Land, Lutener took his place, but when he opened the loophole shutter he was shot through the head; within twenty minutes the sniper had claimed four victims. [Lutener is buried at Essex Farm, I B 4.]

While snipers clinically targeted their victim, artillery shells dispensed death and destruction in a more random manner. About 10 am on 11 April hostile artillery, evidently registering their guns, shelled the front line from E28, on the right of 12/King's Liverpool, to D22, held by 7/Duke of Cornwall's Light Infantry (7/DCLI). At 4.00 pm a fairly intense bombardment fell on the front line and rear areas, including Dawson City, Headingly Lane, The Nile, Lancashire Post and Skipton Post. Two hours later, the shelling increased in intensity at Skipton Post, which suffered

A culvert boarded over makes a good battalion headquarters near Boesinghe. Men of the 1/5 York and Lancaster Regiment were in residence on this occasion.

badly, for the line ran almost into the point of the German salient known to the British as Caesar's Nose. As an attack looked imminent, 61 Brigade headquarters notified division of the intensity and coverage of the shelling, support battalions were ordered to 'Stand To' and the remaining men and machine-guns were ordered up to the canal bank. Believing an attack would centre on D22 (forward of Dawson City), the artillery opened up with shrapnel on the enemy parapet opposite D22.

Around 7.15 pm a rocket shot up from E27; the GOC noticed the red parachute rocket, but there was doubt whether it was an SOS signal. In reply, Brigade HQ fired a similar rocket, with the intention of confirming if the first rocket was indeed an SOS and also showing the front line their message was seen. While attempts to clarify the meaning of the pyrotechnics proceeded, about fifty Germans attacked E28, but their angle of approach allowed them to be enfiladed and they were almost wiped out by Lewis gun and rifle fire, whilst a small party, who occupied a crater in the old E29 trench were bombed out. During the attack, a second group rose from their trenches and advanced, a machine-gun jammed and therefore this advance was checked by artillery and rifle fire. At 7.30 pm a SOS message was sent to the artillery and the response was satisfactory. At 7.50 pm the Liaison Post Officer requested the French to fire on the *Cinq Chemin* crossroads and Köln Farm. The French duly supplied an effective barrage.

The heavily cut up ground made it difficult for the British bombers to reach the enemy but it also slowed down the enemy. When the time came for the Duke of Cornwalls to use their rifles, many jammed owing to the wet and mud thrown up by trench mortars. The reinforcements from Skipton Post arrived up a well-concealed trench to join those manning E27 and E28; the late arrivals had no such problems with clogged rifles.

About forty Germans advanced from C.14.a.4.2 (near Essen Farm) and headed directly for the bombing post to the right of E26. No trench existed for almost a hundred yards and some of the raiders turned off on seeing this gap between E25 and E26. About five Germans managed to pass the remains of the trench in E26 and captured two bombers in a bombing post, whilst they dug out a sergeant buried by a shell blast. Within a minute of their entry, an NCO challenged the infiltrators, thought to be returning bombers from a cut off bombing post. A German replied in faltering English, 'Hands up'! Instead, the sergeant bombed them out. Other Germans occupied a shell crater in front of, and between, E25 and E26, but were dispersed under withering fire from E25. During the attacks a fifteen strong enemy party crawled up close to S32, prior to rushing the old British trench to the left of the post. Faced with a fusillade of rifle, machine-gun fire and bombs, the raiders scattered to the relative safety

A Boesinghe street in 1916.

of nearby ditches; a patrol ordered out to tackle the raiders found no trace of them. Throughout the raid, shells and trench mortars continued to batter D22, where the posts, despite being unfinished, were connected up. This allowed the men to move laterally when they saw incoming trench mortars and thus minimised the casualties. The expected attack never troubled this section and the situation gradually quietened down by around 9.45 pm.

The War Diary casualties for 12/Kings mentions two officers wounded, three other ranks killed and twenty-two wounded. The 7/DCLI casualties were one dead, and one wounded officer, twenty other ranks killed, forty-two wounded and four missing. As an indication of enemy losses, some thirty German dead lay in front of the E27 and E28 parapets.

The trench rumours of an impending divisional relief began to gain some credibility amongst the ranks when junior officers became pre-occupied with balancing the books with regard to the precise quantity of trench stores. In true military fashion, the assortment of waders, grenades and other paraphernalia of war had to be accounted for before officially handing over to the stores to an incoming division. Components of the 20th (Light) Division were relieved by the 6th Division in mid April, and faced the same welcoming reception as their predecessors. In common with other zones, the trenches forward of Turco Farm were 'in a state of incredible disrepair… isolated posts, mere sections of trench that by good fortune had escaped annihilation'.

Throughout 19 April sporadic shelling niggled away at the forlorn defences, until suddenly increasing in tempo at around 5.00 pm. Two hours later, a green rocket soared up from the enemy lines near Morteldje Estaminet, and on cue the guns increased their elevation; shells now fell upon and around the support trenches of Clifford Tower and The Willows and also Vicars Lane communication trench. Field grey clad troops advanced in an earnest attempt to seize objectives previously denied them. By 8.30 pm they had gained, from companies of 8/Bedfordshires, D20, D21, Willow Walk, Ducks Bill, S18 and the adjacent S18A.

Companies of 1/Kings Shropshire Light Infantry were in reserve at Chateau des Trois Tours, from where they provided large working parties for Threadneedle Street (C.21d, 27.b) communication trench, in the Forward Cottage sector. Already A and B Companys were on the east canal bank, B and C Company, less two platoons, now joined them, whilst 2/York and Lancaster left the canal for the support lines. In the early hours of 20 April, one company of 8/Bedfords and two from the York and Lancaster attempted a counter attack. In the darkness and amid unfamiliar trenches, the company of Bedfords believed they had attained their objectives of S18A and Willow Walk; but they were in Gowthorpe Road. Both York and Lancaster companies entered D21 and D20, but were driven back to the far left of D21. The Brigadier commanding cancelled a second attack and instead the lost ground was shelled throughout Friday 21 April in preparation for a night attack by 1/KSLI, currently held in reserve.

The Shropshire Light Infantry Counter Attack

The attack involved three companys. B Company, led by Captain H S Collins, would advance on the right, A Company, Captain T C N Hall, in the centre, and half of C Company on the left. D Company and the remainder of C Company were held in reserve. An hour after sunset on Good Friday the sky clouded over and rain fell in torrents, flooding trenches, turning craters into ponds and the ground into a quagmire. At 10 pm, to coincide with the Shropshires scheduled time of advance, three brief preliminary barrages descended upon the lost positions.

Forty-five minutes later than intended, due to the state of the ground and a pitch-black night, Captain Collin's, B Company advanced from the Boundary Road end of Clifford Tower trench. Two platoons advanced towards their objectives of Morteldje Estaminet and S18a. They took two hours to cross 200 yards of ground. Enfilading heavy rifle and machine-gun fire from the left ripped into the party but they stoically pressed on to S18a, reaching the objective about 1.30 am. The new occupants rapidly made contact with the 2/York and Lancasters to their right, at Algerian Cottage. A group of bombers, led by Company Sergeant Major S Evans, gallantly progressed as far as the southern end of Willow Walk, expecting to link in the centre with A Company but which as yet had been unable to advance. Two bombing posts and a Lewis gun were established in the trench and an extra bombing post near Algerian Cottage. Captain Collins ordered B Company to consolidate their positions along the lines of the obliterated S18a. 'You've got to help consolidate this trench', observed an officer. 'Consolidate what? … This porridge!' came the reply. As the artillery was still bombarding Morteldje Estaminet, Collins wisely postponed an attack on their other objective. Philip Gibbs of the *Daily Telegraph* reported:

> *A few fell into shell craters and drowned. Some were so caught and stuck by the mud that they could not get free nor move a yard. The assaulting companies, all struggling like this, lost touch with each other in the darkness but pressed on independently to their objectives. The men on the right [B Company], or as many as could keep together, rushed the enemy's trench at half past one in the morning, and took possession of it in spite of heavy rifle, grenade and machine-gun fire from the enemy's support trenches.*

The Shropshires counter attack near Morteldje Estaminet/Turco Farm.

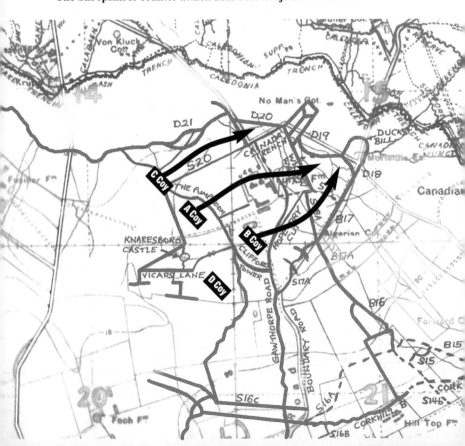

The hundred strong force of A Company, commanded by Captain Hall, after much difficulty, belatedly reached their start point near the Turco Farm stronghold, from where they were to re-take Willow Walk and the Ducks Bill. The company delayed the attack until the 2 am arrival of C Company, who were to attack on their left. Through knee-deep mud, A Company advanced, attracting heavy fire as they passed Turco Farm. Wounded men suffocated in the mud and a new trench dug by the Germans, some thirty yards forward of Willow Walk, added to the difficulties. Fortunately, the enemy withdrew on the approach of A Company, who swept past over the new trench and rushed Willow Walk, filling the air with loud cheers. The few enemy who had not fled the trench were despatched by bomb and bayonet. After consolidating their position, Lieutenant Alec Leith Johnston led about twenty-five men in a successful assault on the Ducks Bill.

Simultaneous to the centre company attack, the two platoons of C Company, now regrouped after becoming scattered in the rain and darkness, advanced on the left, intending to re-gain and then establish a ten-man post at D20, D21, and a fifteen strong post at the junction of S20 and Canada Trench. The only methods of advancing in some places on the left was either to crawl frog-wise, pushing the rifle before them, or else wade with the rifle above the head. Lieutenant Fox's men, after difficulties negotiating wire near S20, came under fire from their objectives, D20 and D21, until their twenty-five opponents withdrew.

As dawn pierced the 22 April sky, the Germans gathered by No Man's Cottage for a counter attack. They advanced into the sights of the A Company Lewis gun. Lieutenant Johnston directed the repulse, continually staying on open ground, until he was shot dead. Meanwhile bombers from A Company blasted their way towards a machine-gun and thirty Germans sited in S18. The occupants retired in the direction of Morteldje, only to be cut up by the rifles of B Company.

A simultaneous dawn attack on C Company got within thirty yards of D20, before recoiling from the bombs and small arms fire. Attempts to infiltrate along a trench at the union of D20 and 21 also came to no avail. Between 6.00 and 7.00 am, during a retaliatory bombardment, the battalion's commanding officer Lieutenant Colonel Luard, was fatally wounded by a shrapnel bullet to the head; despite evacuation to the CCS at Lijssenthoek, he died on 24 April.

The Times reported some instances of the bravery exhibited during the attack:

A lance corporal spent six and a half hours, from 4.00 am to 10.30, getting a wounded man back from a distance of 600 yards. He carried him at first, till wounded in the shoulder; then dragged and pushed him through the mud, being, after daylight, all the time under heavy fire, and when he got him in was in himself in a state of complete exhaustion. A private, after being wounded in the knee, managed to crawl into the German trench and refused to leave because we had insufficient strength, as he thought, to hold it. He stayed there, helping to repulse two counter attacks, for thirty-six hours; and then had to be carried out on a stretcher. Another private held a sap successfully against a counter attack single-handed. One officer went on directing the attack with one arm literally hanging by a shred. A sergeant spent two hours on the following day digging a wounded man out of the mud in daylight, being sniped at the whole time. A private in the RAMC attended to between thirty and forty wounded men in the open, being himself wounded in the head while doing it. He went on, and afterwards organised parties for bringing in isolated wounded left in the mud.

During their two-day occupancy the enemy had dug a fresh trench, fitted iron loopholes throughout the captured trenches, and ran several communication trenches to their new acquisitions; they obviously intended to stay. However, the Shropshires captured and held their positions, albeit at the expense of four officers killed (including Luard) and five wounded. The regimental history also reports twenty-two other ranks killed, 135 wounded and six missing. The battalion was relieved on the night of 22/23 April.

Graves within the quagmire of what had been Boesinghe Wood.

Colonel Luard is buried in Lijssenthoek Military Cemetery (V A 23); Lieutenant Johnson had an interesting career. Johnston originally joined the Artists' Rifles and saw service at the front. He later received a commission in the KSLI; he was wounded a few months prior to his death. He had a long association with *Punch* and, during the war, he contributed many wry articles under such titles as *At the back of the front* and *At the front*. His grave is in Essex Farm, II. Q. 19.

During spring little of note occurred in the northern sector of the Salient possibly due to Allied attention being focussed on the preparations for the 'Big Push'. During May 2/Durham Light Infantry rotated in the lines near E23 to E26, Dawson City and canal bank. Their War Diary differed little from other battalions, whose recording of the monotonous existence in the line varied from, 'A quiet day with some shelling' to:

May 23rd. About 1.00 am a party of about thirty Germans was seen approaching our trenches. Bombs were thrown and rifle fire brought to bear on this party; it was dispersed. Gas alert received at 4.55 pm. A German aeroplane dropped two bombs on east canal bank at 6.35 pm. At dusk a small enemy party was observed walking along their parapet, one was shot. A patrol went out from left to reconnoitre trenches, which had been evacuated by a previous division and found them unoccupied but full of water. Casualties, one other rank killed. A draft of thirty other ranks arrived.

1/West Yorkshires, completed their relief of the Durham soldiers by 12.40 am on 25 May. The battalion occupied dugouts on the canal bank. About 11.30 am, enemy shells strafed the road to the north of Marengo Farm, and five minutes later shells rained down on the canal bank. A dugout occupied by B Company received a direct hit; no one died, but nineteen men received shrapnel wounds. Throughout May, when 2/Durham LI had held the line, the war of attrition had claimed nine dead and fifty-two wounded.

Evidently, the dugouts were less secure than they appeared and they offered more of a psychological protection against heavy shells than a physical defensive shield. The dugouts certainly left a lot to be desired. Cyril George Dennys served as an officer with 212 Siege Battery Royal Garrison Artillery, and later recalled his first experience of canal bank accommodation:

Billets suggest you are living with civilians somewhere but you are not. All billets meant in the artillery were places where you rested some way behind the battery station and a little bit out of the line of fire. So we came along and there was a huge bank, with a lot of holes dug in it, these were lined with semi circular elephant iron,

By 1916 a massive crater existed within the churchyard.

and that was were they were living. I crawled into a hole vacated by a corporal on leave and spent the night there. The next morning a sergeant major suggested my men dig a dugout for me. So I took my men and we started to dig a hole for me despite the shells bursting. I hadn't the least idea if they were lethal or not, you heard a roar, a burst of mud, smoke, fumes and so on. Whether they were going to do us any harm or not I didn't know, and none of the men who hadn't been out before knew either, so we hoped we were not going to be hit. I later discovered they were miles away and of no possible harm. We made a one man dugout, four feet wide and eight feet deep, with a roof of corrugated elephant iron, with trench boards on the floor, sandbags acted as pillows for the head. There was also a trestle that you could place a stretcher on or, if you could get hold of some netting or rabbit wire, make up a rough bed, I've had worse.

The above artillery officer was just one minor cog in the British military machine and one of the legion who received little or no recognition of their role in the Great War for Civilisation. While the passing of the majority of fallen men receive little or no recognition in divisional histories, for instance the *History of the 6th Division* provides only a brief summary of events, yet it goes out of its way to honour a man dubbed 'The Admiral'. Lieutenant Cyril Aldin Smith was originally an owner-driver, in charge of a convoy of buses with the Royal Naval Division at Antwerp, until the withdrawal. In October 1914 he drove an officer to his unit in the front line, where Smith managed to get himself attached to the 6th Division's headquarters. Commissioned into the RNVR on 11 September 1915, he experimented in the front line with bullet-proof shields mounted on wheels, a form of embryonic tank. Whilst participating in a small three-man pattern raid near Forward Cottage (C21.b.8.5), he eagerly preceded the shield by several yards, and received a shell splinter to his neck. The name of 'Admirals', given to the road past Crossroads Farm and Forward Cottage, commemorates the incident.

Lieutenant C A Smith RNVR (The Admiral).

Later 'The Admiral' turned his attention to Bangalore Torpedoes, an apparatus for destroying, by explosion, enemy wire. He trained his authorised group, the 6th Division Shield Party, in their use, and joined them in numerous raids, one of which earned him the DSO, gazetted in April 1916. His father wrote, 'He came home to England, to receive his decoration from the King in early June and returned about the 7th June'. On 9 June, whilst participating in a 9/Norfolk raiding party, attempting to destroy an observation post, the group became surrounded by Germans. The thirty-nine year old 'Admiral' was wounded and reported missing; he was never seen again. Addenda panel fifty-seven of

Admirals Road viewed from Morteleje Estaminet crossroads present-day.

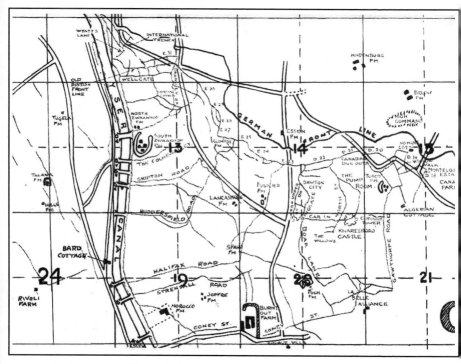

A sketch map of the principal trenches in the northern sector of the Salient.

the Menin Gate commemorates the death of Lieutenant Cyril Aldin Smith, DSO.

The Admiral was just one of almost 11,000 casualties sustained by the 6th Division during their eighteen months in the Salient. Shortly after Smith's death, the division received orders to prepare to entrain south for their role in the 'Big Push'. Among those heading south were 11/Essex and 8/Bedfords, relieved on 16 June by 1/Irish Guard, who now covered the Ypres to Pilkem road, with supports at Lancashire Farm.

Lancashire Farm, where the pleasant smell of a soup kitchen fought unavailingly against the stench of the old farm pool, the sickly stink of blue clay ladled about by mysterious tunnellers, and the universal trench combination smell of brazier, sandbag, chloride of lime, creosol, latrines and fried bacon.

1/8 Irish Guards' Battalion headquarters were established in loose bricks and mud on the canal bank.

The trenches were bad, only Skipton Road was moderately dry and the parapets were low, thin and non existent in parts. As the poppies and thistles grew brightest and tallest around the fringes of craters, and as shell holes meant cover, all patrols in No Man's Land used them as cover. German snipers also had perfect cover, for some 250 yards from the front

106

were five dugouts formerly in British hands. Now extensively encircled by wire, interwoven with long grass, 'Canadian dugouts' provided excellent coverage for the snipers. On the first day, snipers killed two guardsmen, another died of wounds and four were wounded. On 18 June officer patrols crawled out to inspect the enemy wire. Second Lieutenant Lee was wounded in the leg and carried back by 3836 Corporal Redmond; the officer later died of gangrene. On the return journey an officer ran by error into wire and he and his orderly had to fight their way back. One man died, another received wounds, in addition to the fatally wounded officer.

Three days at Elverdinghe followed. On returning to the line on the 24th, a sniper killed one man and wounded another and two days later snipers added another four to their tally. Next day Lieutenant F L Pusch DSO and his orderly set off to pick up a wounded man within a trench; the same sniper's bullet killed both of the rescuers. Despite the sniper's attention, Private Carroll succeeded in dragging the wounded man and the officer's body under cover, for which he received the Military Medal. 1/Irish Guards casualties for a twelve-day tour of the line, including only three days in the front line, were three officers and forty-seven other ranks killed or wounded.

An Irish Guards intelligence raid

2/Irish Guards on 28 June had their headquarters and two companies at the relatively unscathed Elverdinge chateau, whilst two companies were in the canal bank dugouts. Lieutenant F Pym, a bold, daring and steady

A Boesinghe street in 1916.

officer, selected volunteers from each company for a thirty man and one sergeant raiding party. Their mission appears to have been the location of 'gas machines', for three Royal Engineer gas experts joined the party. The raid, on the evening of 2 July, would follow a twenty minutes bombardment by howitzers and trench mortars. After ten minutes the Stokes mortars were to join in and, at 10.00 pm, the guns would lift and form another barrage, whilst Stokes mortars dealt with the flanks. It was a clear summer night, so the men were instructed to leave their jackets on, as their shirts would make them too conspicuous.

After ten minutes of shelling, the enemy guns replied with a retaliatory barrage on the Nile support trench. There was still sufficient light to see the German parapets as British raiders went over the top. They attracted machine-gun fire yet reached the enemy wire, previously cut by the bombardment. Lieutenant Pym led the charge into the enemy trench, turned left with a handful of men, reached the door of a machine-gun dugout and entered. Inside, two men manning their deadly weapon were dealt with and one became a prisoner. In accordance with the attack plan, bombers took up position to the left and right. Centrally within the captured trench, German bombers attacked from the junction of a communication trench. The British seized five prisoners; one unmanageable prisoner was shot and four were escorted back to the lines, but German shellfire killed two of them. The engineers unsuccessfully searched the trench for apparatus, whilst a Royal Engineer gathered documents; however, these were lost when he was killed. Sergeant Austen was hit, and fell in the German wire. One of the raiders stayed with him, before dragging him back to the British lines. At 10.10 pm Pym blew his horn, signalling the retirement, the returning men scrambling over the British parapet, falling victim to machine gun and shellfire and here the majority of the casualties occurred. Hostile shellfire continued until 11.00 pm, hindering the overground evacuation of casualties to Lancashire Farm. Lieutenant Pym failed to return to the British trenches and he and a dozen others died on 2 July, whilst another guardsman died of his wounds next day. Lieutenant F L M Pym, and Privates T Cassidy, P Donovan, W Horan, M Maher and M McHale are commemorated on panel eleven of the Menin Gate. The graves of Privates M Kelleher (Kelliher in the CWGC records), J Martin, F McGuire, P McQuinn, J O'Connell and P O'Sullivan are to be found in Essex Farm. Private P Nolan has a 3 July date of death on his headstone at V A 28 Poelcapelle British Cemetery. Private Casey died of wounds the day after the raid and lies in Lijssenthoek Military Cemetery, VIII B 44.

The battalion's period in the Salient concluded at the end of the month, when they headed for the Somme battlefields.

Enter the Dragon

In early July 1916, the blood of the 38th (Welsh) Division flowed freely on the Somme at Mametz Wood. Wyn Griffith, of 15th Royal Welsh Fusiliers (RWF), summed up their sacrifice at the infernal wood, 'The flower of young Wales stood up to machine guns with success that astonished all who knew the ground'. However, one chapter in the distinguished history of the division is rarely mentioned, namely their occupation of the canal sector from August 1916 to the days preceding Third Ypres. Major W P Wheldon DSO, RWF gave a graphic record of his new surroundings:

> *The canal itself was shallow with a bottom of slimy filth, strewn with bully beef tins and empty jam tins; some derelict barges there were too, one proudly named the* Duke of Wellington, *all of which only made it abundantly clear that it was no longer a canal but a drain in which rats, of all living things, found life and pleasure. The stream running parallel to the canal, and called the Yperlee, in times of flood flowed muddy and strong. To behold it in drier seasons it was incredible that any man could have drunk of its waters and lived, but many did or, if they died, the cause was something more drastic, if really less nasty, than its waters.*

A view from the west canal bank, looking towards the German lines.

Little of note beyond the usual routine occurred as autumn approached, but drainage work again appears in work schedules. On 19 October 17/RWF, in the front line at Ealing Trench (C.13.d.14.c), reported trenches collapsing due to the previous days of heavy rain. Working parties now fought against nature in an almost futile attempt to keep front and communication trenches serviceable. John Malcolm Lawrence Grover served as battalion Lewis gun officer with 1/KSLI and also served with 2/KSLI:

> *I spent a lot of time in the Salient, where the water level is just below the surface, and when it rains the*

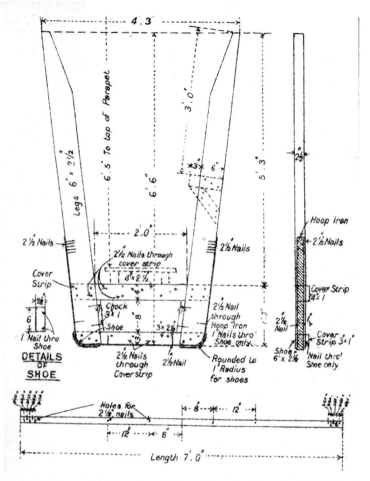

Sketch of the construction of an A Frame from the Manual of Field Works.

whole thing is just one field of mud, so all the defences have to be built up. Which means you not only have to build them up with sandbags, you have to revet them very strongly. We had things called 'A frames', in the form of an inverted A with a trace across to allow a drain below, and that was the inside of the trench, these were fitted in and were revetted inside.

Away from the waterlogged trenches, Elverdinghe Chateau, despite attracting the attention of aerial torpedoes and whiz-bangs, remained structurally sound. Although the furniture and pictures, along with the glazing, had long gone, its high, stale smelling, rooms still offered decent shelter. On 28 October the officers of the Liverpool Scottish invited guests to a celebratory dinner at the chateau to mark the award of the Victoria Cross to the battalion medical officer, Noel Godfrey Chavasse MC, gazetted two days previously for actions at Guillemont during the

Battle of the Somme. Shortly before his death on 4 August 1917, 'The Doc's' bravery during the opening days of the Third Battle of Ypres merited the posthumous awarding of a bar (ie a second VC), a unique double award during the conflict, as no other serviceman received two such awards for Great War gallantry. His poppy adorned grave, one of the most regularly visited in the Salient, is in Brandhoek New Military Cemertery, Vlamertinghe, III B 15.

Noel Godfrey Chavasse.

Apart from the British taking over a section of the canal front line towards Boesinghe in December, little of significance occurred until the night of 23 December when 17/RWF relieved 10/South Wales Borderers (SWB) in the line at Boesinghe Chateau (B.11.b.8.4.). On their left flank stood the 3rd Battalion of The 2nd Regiment Chasseurs à Pied, while to the RWF's right 10/Rifle Brigade held the line. At 2 am next morning the enemy launched a one hour intensive heavy and medium trench mortar bombardment. The onslaught initially fell to the Fusiliers' right but gradually swept down upon their positions, pulverising the front trenches, support lines and communication trenches forward of company headquarters. The Village Lines were similarly strafed by high explosive and shrapnel shells, whilst rifle grenades rained down on the machine-gun swept front line parapets.

The storm of steel ensured British sentries took cover, allowing an enemy raiding party to cross the canal by raft, probably opposite the bombing post on the railway bridge. The Germans overpowered the post and entered the front line by B.12.b.4.4. During the ensuing chaos a British Lewis gun post sited fifty yards to the left was obliterated by a trench mortar whilst another Lewis gun crew, some fifty yards to the right, under the orders of its commander, split up. Two men moved to the left, but the corporal, Lewis gun, and three men headed in the opposite direction towards the bridge; it was a pitch-black night and the quartet walked straight into the raiding party. The four men were probably taken prisoner by the Germans who, having achieved the objective of their intelligence gathering raid, returned by rafts to the opposite bank.

As a result of the raid on the British line the RWF casualties were two officers and five men wounded. A further two non commissioned officers and ten men were originally posted as missing; however four of these men were discovered to have been killed and buried by the bombardment.

The German raid dispelled all illusions of the canal being an effective obstacle to an enemy intent on bridging the break in the Railway Bridge or rafting across the canal unseen during a protective barrage. The line, previously held for a month by the 39th Division, was evidently flawed. Consequently the following night, which was Christmas Eve, the sector's system of defence underwent re-organisation.

The arrival of Christmas once again induced the Germans to adopt a friendly attitude, regardless of their aggressive raid less than forty-eight hours previously. The War Diary entry for 17/RWF on Christmas Day 1916 noted:

> *In the early hours the enemy showed a desire to be friendly, calling out to our men, 'Good morning Tommy, it is Christmas morning. A Happy Christmas to you. I hope we will both be friends.' They sang English songs, including God Save the King, accompanied by a flute and a concertina. Two of them showed themselves and waved, but withdrew before a shot could be fired at them.*

Throughout Christmas Day British artillery steadily bombarded the German lines. On Boxing Day, following a relief by 10/South Wales Borderers, 17/RWF proceeded to support billets at Bleuet Farm.

A trench map with names overlaid relevant to the events on 11 July 1917.

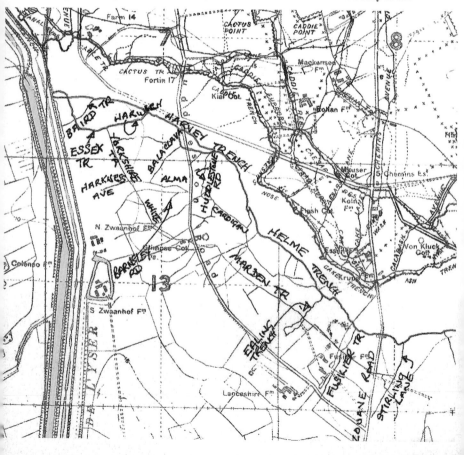

Chapter Six

BRITISH CAPTURE THE
CANAL'S EAST BANK FACING BOESINGHE

On the outbreak of hostilities, some of Britain's military leaders had confidently predicted the European War would be over by Christmas 1914. Instead, the war of attrition extended beyond its fourth Christmas. Now, with the period of 'Peace on earth' firmly behind them, the Germans facing Boesinghe celebrated the New Year of 1917, by using a heavy minenwerfer, sited in the ruins of a steam mill (B.6.d.4.0. 3.5), to create enormous explosions in the village and surroundings. The lines were now held by the 39th Division, whose 116 Brigade contained 11/Royal Sussex, the battalion of Second Lieutenant Edmund Blunden. This junior officer composed many poems based on two years' trench experiences. In 1928 he published his classic book *Undertones of War*, in which Blunden records his first impressions of Boesinghe:

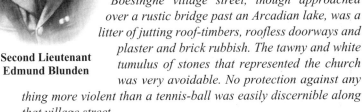

The burnt chateau was only a useless case, the battalion headquarters was an iron vault in an outbuilding, with fragile huts and coop-like sandbag annexes obviously clustered round. Boesinghe village street, though approached over a rustic bridge past an Arcadian lake, was a litter of jutting roof-timbers, roofless doorways and plaster and brick rubbish. The tawny and white tumulus of stones that represented the church was very avoidable. No protection against any thing more violent than a tennis-ball was easily discernible along that village street...

**Second Lieutenant
Edmund Blunden**

Shelters concealed in the rubble of Boesinghe church.

A bitterly cold spell set in during early February, producing a foot deep layer of ice upon the canal. Each night bombers broke up the ice to prevent the Germans crossing over the frozen water. The frozen earth proved almost impossible to dig unless Royal Engineers blasted the soil's surface. These measures continued until mid February, when a gradual thaw set in. About this time, 15/RWF were employed in collecting 600 sandbags of discarded tins but their efforts made little impression, for every shell revealed still more. This foraging activity appears to have been a passion of a particular brigadier, who assigned a part of Headingley Lane trench as a dump site for the thousands of collected beef and jam tins discarded by the entrenched armies.

On 9 February, a raiding party of five officers and 150 men from 14/RWF went to E Camp for training. Unusually, five officers and 174 other ranks from 10 (Liverpool Scottish) King's Liverpool, of 55th Division, took over the 14/RWF's vacated place in the line. To attach a company of one battalion to another, even in its own brigade, was unusual; the attachment to another division, except in the confusion of battle, is extremely unusual. The records of the Liverpool Scottish contain no explanation for this temporary attachment. Captain L G Wall, with his V Company of 120 men, held the right sub sector, while fifty men from X Company entered the left sub sector. During the Liverpool Scottish's six day attachment, six men were killed and five were wounded by shellfire. The Liverpool Scottish dead were Lance Corporal A Murdock [or Murdoch] and Privates F E Collinson, F G Evans, J H G Gorson [or Gosson] and F Peaston; the four men lie alongside each other at Bard Cottage Cemetery II B 16 to II B 19; Private Reginald Carter died of wounds and lies in Mendinghem Cemetery II A 9, close to Private Peaston (II A 20), who was fatally wounded during the same bombardment.

Serving in the battalion was Sergeant Frank G Evans, a pre-war civil servant stationed in London and then Doncaster. The Birkenhead man joined the Liverpool Scottish, where he rapidly rose to the rank of sergeant. He successfully passed the bombing course and, due to his ability to teach in a pleasant and effective manner, he was appointed bombing instructor. Sergeant Evans arrived in France on 3 January 1917; six weeks later he was dead. His officer wrote

> He was one of seven men occupying a post in the first line of trenches, when a shell dropped in their midst killing four of them and wounding the other three. He showed great courage during a severe bombardment prior to his death. You have no idea how he will be missed by his numerous friends and comrades...

The 14/RWF raiding party, led by Lieutenant Harold Sydney Ormsby, consisted of Second Lieutenants Stork, Williams, Lloyd and James plus 145 other ranks. At 3.19 am on 18 February the raiding party penetrated the enemy front line, north of Essen Farm (C.14.a.3.4.), where a heavy trench mortar and artillery barrage inflicted heavy casualties. Lieutenant Ormsby was an early casualty, but despite his severe wounds displayed great gallantry by encouraging the men forward. No progress was made due to the barrage. After a hellish fifteen minutes in the enemy line, the party withdrew, in the process suffering further casualties from machine guns and trench mortars.

Twice wounded, Lieutenant Ormsby MID succumbed to his wounds next day and lies in Bard Cottage Cemetery II D 3. His headstone states he was a Captain and also, erroneously, that he died on 18 February. Second Lieutenant Enoch Lewis James was killed, he is commemorated on the Panel 22 of the Menin Gate. Second Lieutenant Williams was wounded. *Soldiers Died* lists fifteen other rank fatalities.

Possibly to maintain their offensive spirit or in reply to the British raid, the Germans, in conjunction with an artillery bombardment, attacked a 14/RWF held trench at 2.45 am on 25 February. The Royal Artillery took fifteen minutes to respond to the SOS signal from the British front line; this delay allowed the enemy raiding party to return to their own lines unscathed with a RWF prisoner. The German shelling killed Captain P F Craddock, Lieutenant W J Williams and Second Lieutenant Stanley Jones and ten private soldiers, a further nine other ranks were wounded. The three officer casualties lie in Bard Cottage cemetery II A 1 to II A 3. Nine

Due to the destruction of the lock gates the canal drained away.

of the soldiers killed also lie in Bard Cottage, their graves can be found between and inclusive of II D 1 to II D 21. Another victim of the raid, Private Percy Moore, lies in Mendinghem Cemetery II B 1.

Apart from such minor incidents and shelling during the British troops 'sit and be hit' occupancy of the Boesinghe line, little occurred during the first quarter of the year. Nothing appears to have escaped the German gunners who, in early March, whiled away their time shelling screens fixed to trees along the Boesinghe-Ypres road (B.18d.6.0) near Hulls Farm. Throughout the spring months, night fighting patrols continued to take the war to the German wire. In the quest for information even the most unlikely opportunities were pursued. The 17/RWF War Diary entry for 25 March records: At morning 'Stand To' a dog within our wire was shot and brought in, but there were no marks of identification.

The 38th (Welsh) Division, while holding the line from the Ypres-Pilckem Road to Boesinghe, spent late May and early June digging assembly trenches in readiness for the summer attack. In places they advanced the line some 300 yards, reducing No Man's Land to 200 yards. The enemy paid scant attention to their activities, seen as a method of drawing attention away from the imminent attack upon the Messines Ridge.

A Flanders based German infantryman poses for the camera, 20 May 1917.

A trench raid by the 16th Welch battalion

In late May preparations were in hand for a 16/Welch raid on the enemy trenches, intended 'to capture or kill any enemy encountered and to obtain identification'. The raid, opposite Boesinghe village, involved two parties of men, one officer, a sergeant and twelve men, plus two men who remained on the western canal bank. Number One section consisted of an officer, four bayonet men and one bomber, equipped with a dozen Mills bombs. The same applied to Number Two section, except they were in the charge of a sergeant. Most of the riflemen carried loaded rifles (ten rounds) plus twenty more rounds and two bombs. Orders stated that these were to be carried in their pockets, all marks of identification were removed from uniforms and equipment and, ominously, orders stipulated that each man should write his name on paper and carry it in his pocket.

The original plan involved a silent raid. However, as the night of 5/6 June was brightly lit by the moon, the raiders would attack during a trench mortar bombardment arranged at the last minute. But first they had to cross the canal. Some eighteen inches of canal water covered an equal depth of mud, capable of supporting a load if the weight was distributed evenly across the surface. To facilitate the crossing, two special roll mats (60 by 5 and 50 by 5 feet) would span the divide.

To deceive the enemy, short bursts of Stokes mortar were fired at the German front line at 6 and 11 pm. At 12.30 am machine-guns fired on pre-ordained targets, whilst trench mortars fell on positions away from the British entry point. At 12.39 am both parties set off simultaneously, Party A from B634G, the other from B12G 7005. Opposite both points were enormous gaps in the German wire. The lead man of each party bravely walked on the mat, unrolling it before him, and secured it to the opposite canal bank. The mats allowed six to eight men to cross, albeit knee deep in water.

Each party acted independently. The Northern Party, led by Second Lieutenant Arnold O Jones of A Company, entered and searched forty yards of the enemy trench, described as six feet deep, revetted with brushwood and in good repair. Island traverses were numerous, one bay was wired and could only be entered by crawling. They found a dugout at B.6.c.40.50, where a sergeant took by surprise three members of 2nd Battalion 388th Landwehr Regiment, attached to 23rd Reserve Division. The men, two Saxons in their early forties and a Polish Reservist stretcher-bearer, became prisoners. With the goal achieved, Second Lieutenant Jones gave the pre-arranged retirement signal of one long blast on a whistle. The British and prisoners safely reached the opposite bank and retracted the roll mat.

The Southern Party fared worse, for they entered the trenches near eight Germans. A fierce fight ensued, Second Lieutenant L R Jones being killed immediately, three men were severely wounded, three others only slightly. The raiders appear to have eliminated the German post for they met no resistance as they extricated their wounded back to their starting point. Pre-occupied with their wounded they abandoned their mission, returning without any information. Each raid lasted a maximum of twenty-minutes.

In recognition of their endeavours Second Lieutenant A Jones received

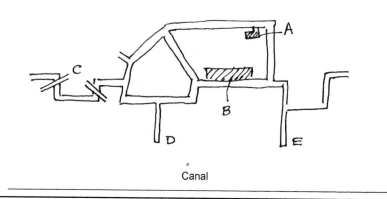

A- Dugout where prisoners were found: concrete for 5 men.

B- Large shelter covered in three foot of earth.

C- Wired Bay.

D- Point of entry.

E.- Sap, snipers posts/Tramway.

A sketch plan of the German position raided on the night of 5/6 June 1917 by the 16th Welch.

the Military Cross, while Sergeant W E Richards, Corporal T B Tobieson, Lance Corporal D J Collier, Privates R H Pugh and W Johnson received the Military Medal.

Meanwhile, planning for an Allied breakout from the Salient were now coming to a head. On 10 June, Sir Hubert Gough's Fifth Army came into the line on the left of the Second Army, occupying the trenches from Observatory Ridge to Boesinghe. General Anthoine's French First Army,

Little now remained of the village.

five days later, relieved the Belgians holding the line from Boesinghe to Nordschoote, south of Dixmuide; and five days later the British relieved the French between St Georges and the North Sea. The stage was now set for the summer offensive, and in order to disguise the movements of thousands of gathering troops, Haig maintained an aggressive attitude from positions south of Ypres.

In the north the raids continued, including one launched at 11.30 pm on 24 June involving one officer and twenty-three other ranks from 13/RWF, ordered to enter the German trench in close proximity to Essen Farm (C.14a.35.35). The raiders encountered three thick belts of enemy barbed wire. The first two consisted of concertina wire mounted on knife rests, which were damaged and trampled down in parts, allowing the British to thread their way through the barriers, only to discover a third barrier, concealed in a hollow in the ground. This extensive and impenetrable entanglement of concertina wire ran parallel with the front line trench and proved impassable to the raiders, especially as the enemy post was occupied. However it did offer an insight into some of the obstacles facing the British in the forthcoming major offensive.

The 38th Division now received notification of its role in the future assault, followed by a transfer from VIII Corps to XIV Corps. At the end of June, the Guards Division relieved the 38th Division, who left to practice assaults on a replica of Pilckem Ridge. Horace Calvert was an underage volunteer who joined 2/6 West Yorks and later transferred to 1/6 West Yorks. Shortly before the battalion went overseas Calvert deserted, returned home to Bradford and enlisted into the Grenadier Guards. Private Calvert described the canal bank accommodation:

They were old dugouts built up and a tremendous height, you were safe in them and there was room for eight or nine men. They were all sandbagged and well kept, but there were holes in the corners where rats came in. The first night we went in hoping to get a good night's sleep, somebody shouted out, 'There's rats'. We woke up and there were rats all over the place, they were after the food we had brought out for breakfast. You see we could not have it after 'Stand To', you were all packed up ready to move out and have a drink if you could. The rats were in corner sandbags. We had to get some candles, in the candle light we took turns to sit up with the old entrenching tool handle, and every time we heard them – bang. They were vicious, the officers spent quite a lot of time shooting them in the canal.

During the first week of July the 51st (Highland) Division deployed units midway between Ypres and Boesinghe in the improbable hope that they might acclimatise, but constant barrages ensured that the new arrivals, already aghast at the deplorable conditions, were kept in a constant state of tension. Nowhere was safe from the remorseless shellfire. Beneath the ruins of shell blasted Turco Farm, the British constructed a deep command post, built with concrete blocks, and associated trenches. Signaller Stanley Bradbury, 1/5 Seaforth Highlanders,

Just before teatime, two trench mortars dropped simultaneously, one on each of the two entrances to the dugout. The result was terrific. The whole of the heavy cement blocks crashed in, burying those under and near them and the dugout was reduced to a heap of dirt and debris. The dugout had been full of men, all sitting on the steps from the top to the bottom, I and two more being at the bottom. We were blown amongst a heap of wreckage onto the floor of the dugout but, beyond the shock, had not suffered any injury, although from the cries and groans of those who had been on the steps it seemed that many were terribly injured. A state of panic then existed, as with intense darkness and the only entrance whereby fresh air could enter the dugout being completely blocked, there appeared to be a grave fear that we should suffocate. ...I then requested all those who were capable of shouting to shout as hard as they could to attract attention... This appeared to be to no avail but after what seemed an eternity (it was really only about fifteen minutes), we heard digging going on at the entrance. Plenty of willing helpers were soon engaged in removing the debris and very soon there was a large hole through which we could see daylight. This gradually became larger and larger until it was possible to wriggle through. By the light, which streamed through the aperture we were able to see what damage had been done. Where there had once been steps, now dead and wounded lay half buried in the debris. With the aid of those outside, we were all in turn extricated, that is those it was possible to extricate, as one or two were pinned under solid blocks of concrete. Once out in the daylight we were able to take note of our casualties; which were three killed and thirty-two wounded out of a total of thirty-eight occupants of the dugout. (See *Passchendaele*, Steel and Hart, p.77.)

Also involved in the preparations for the forthcoming attack were two companies from 1/Lancashire Fusiliers, who arrived on 5 July at the ruins of Rivoli Farm (B24 central), some 400 yards west of the Yser canal. The men sheltered under hedges, almost every one of which housed a 4.5 howitzer battery or two, brought up for the offensive. A few whiz bangs landed in the Lancashire Fusiliers' field and fragments from eight-inch shells filled the air as the Germans attempted to knock out the howitzers. The Fusiliers' companies were engaged in working parties, constructing

Sandbagged shelters believed to be just north of Essex Farm.

emplacements for trench mortars and bringing Livens gas shells from the railhead to the gun pits, no easy task through an hour-long bombardment on the trolley line. One man was killed and six were wounded.

The battalion moved to Hounslow Camp, where they remained until 13 July, when they moved to the canal bank support line, from where they supplied working parties for 123 Field Company RE. The next day D Company, now billeted in a field west of the canal, were shelled, five men died and eighteen were wounded. The graves of the Lancashire Fusiliers are in Bard Cottage cemetery III A 6 to III A 11. On the night of 18 July a severe enemy counter barrage fell on the support trenches and the canal side. A relief by 16/RWF two nights later concluded the Lancashire Fusiliers unremarkable fortnight in the canal zone, yet one officer and twenty-four other ranks were killed; and a further sixty-six other ranks were wounded.

In readiness for their role in the battle of Third Ypres the incoming 38th (Welsh) Division relieved the 29th Division and took up positions to the right of the Guards Division. No sooner had 16/RWF arrived in the front line (Zwanhoff Farm sector) than they sent out a midnight patrol. An officer and ten men crept out to within twenty-fire yards of the enemy wire; here they waited, while the patrol commander and an NCO advanced to the lip of the trench. A German sentry raised the alarm, rifle and revolver shots pierced the night, whilst six or eight bombs passed over British heads. Having located the post, the patrol retired at 1.30 am.

Two nights later, facing Cactus Trench, Sergeant Jones apprehended in the front line (C.7.c.0.6.), an officer claiming to belong to the Royal Garrison Artillery. Evidently, his claims were not *bona fide* for a 14th Battalion officer took charge of the prisoner.

At the start of July, 1/Irish Guards headquarters were based at Bleuet Farm (B10.c.), a half mile east of Elverdinghe, while their men held the sand-bagged west bank trenches. An (allegedly) two-day rest period followed, when the battalion supplied 110 men for nightly front line carrying parties. The battalion resumed front line duties on 11 July, taking up positions in Boesinghe village, with headquarters in the chateau. All day shells fell around the ruined chateau, in the rear of which the Aid Post and headquarters of Number One Company were sited. Battalion headquarters were shelled for thirty minutes and Number Three Company headquarters in the support line received direct hits, forcing the company to abandon the position.

Nothing seemed particularly untoward on the night of 14 July, as a barrage fell on the support lines whilst a box barrage by trench mortars, artillery and machine guns focussed on two platoons of Number Four Company Irish Guards, holding the canal front line. An alert Lewis gunner witnessed the Germans crossing the canal and from the weapon's covered emplacement, sited almost on the canal bed, the gun team poured fire along the length of the canal, scattering the enemy into the darkness and undergrowth. Other Germans rushed over the parapet between two groups of sentries; in the darkness confusion reigned, as opponents were required to make split second decisions on who was friend or foe. Lieutenant Harry Eyre (nineteen years old, according to CWGC) came out of the remnants of a trench and met head on an enemy party. His steel helmet and empty chamber revolver were later discovered, and it transpired the missing officer had been fatally wounded. (Harry Joseph Bagshawe Eyre lies in Perth Cemetery (China Wall) XVI A 12).

> *The barrage blew the men about like withered leaves, covered them with mud, plastered them with bits of sandbags, and gapped, as it seemed, fathoms of trench at a stroke, while enemy machine guns scissored back and forth across the gap.*

Shortly after the raid began the enemy melted away into the darkness and returned to their lines. A captured prisoner, devoid of any identification, claimed he belonged to the *Schleswig* Regiment. The Irish Guards, who suffered only three casualties, attributed the raid to an identification foray. The Germans returned to their lines with disturbing information, for they had seen what they believed were mineshafts. But, the raiders' 'mineshafts' were really chambers created by 173 Tunnelling Company

A trench on the site of Boesinghe station, wrecked goods wagons are visible on the right of the horizon.

for the storage of bridging material needed for the impending attack.

The five feet by four feet closely timbered tunnels penetrated the bank for quite some depth. They were really mined dug outs, created in late June 1917. At least three existed, between B.12.a.85.70 to 70.95; these were occupied by the Warwicks, RHA Signals and 173rd Company Royal Engineers. More tubes existed between B.12d.85.70 to B.5.d.70.95 but running sand denied the Guards Division mined dug outs in Wallkrantz Trench (28 NW2 B.12.d.05.00). Aware of their own sappers' mining activities the enemy expected the British to act likewise, further fuelling the rumours of an imminent mine explosion.

Meticulous Preparations for the Battle of Pilckem Ridge

The intelligence gained from prisoners and patrol work, combined with photographs taken by the Royal Flying Corps, allowed an accurate replica of the Pilckem battle zone to be created. While in reserve, units in the northern Salient assigned to the forthcoming Third Ypres offensive entrained at Elverdinghe for Proven and then marched to Herzeele. There they practiced attacking formations, including pillbox elimination training; each man learnt his individual role in the battle and his company's objectives. The training reduced the risk of failure but crossing the Yser Canal still posed a serious obstacle to any infantry advance.

During the preparations Royal Engineers repaired or constructed roads destined to connect with four of seventeen new bridges that would span the canal on the eve of the attack. On 24 July, 187 Tunnelling Company from Third Army commenced work on the west side of the canal (B.6.c.2.7.) to remove the parts of the bank obstructing the new roadways. The War Diary explains how this was achieved. Instead of labouriously excavating the vast earth mounds, the Engineers used Wombat Drills with eight-inch diameter augers to bore into the bank. The parallel boreholes for each cut were positioned nine feet below the upper surface and only took a few hours to complete. They were then charged with sufficient explosive to blast a channel through the bank. A thirty-foot tall Poplar tree on the canal bank at B.6.c.2.7.9 (north of the Bois des Crapouillots), where a new road would link with a pontoon bridge, created difficulties, yet six inch diameter holes some thirty four feet long were bored in a few hours. Next day, attempts to bore five holes at B.6.c.8.0, in total about ninety feet, proved unsatisfactory. On 26 July, two other trials, thirty feet along the bank, were also unsuccessful, possibly due to brickwork within the mounds. Both forty-foot long bores remained unfinished until the morning of 31 July and, in common with the others, were lined with tubes.

The original intention was to use Ammonal explosive charges, contained in five feet long by five and a half inch diameter canisters, but

Sketch of canal tubes.

21-6-17 Started canal tubes from B.12.d.85.70 to B.5.d.70.95

SKETCH OF TUBE NUMBER ONE

Dimensions 5' x 4' close timbering

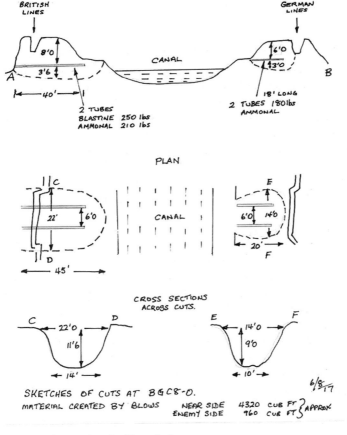

BRITISH
LINES

GERMAN
LINES

8'0
3'6

CANAL

6'0
13'0

A

B

40'

2 TUBES
BLASTINE 250 lbs
AMMONAL 210 lbs

18' LONG
2 TUBES 180lbs
AMMONAL

PLAN

C

22'   6'0

CANAL

E
6'0 14'0

45'

D

20'

F

CROSS SECTIONS
ACROSS CUTS.

C   22'0   D

11'6

14'

E   14'0   F

9'0

10'

SKETCHES OF CUTS AT B G C8-O.
MATERIAL CREATED BY BLOWS   NEAR SIDE   4320 CUB FT ⎫ APPROX
                              ENEMY SIDE   960 CUB FT ⎬

6/8/17

A Royal Engineers sketch of bore holes.

these snagged on the rivets of the tubes lining the holes. Instead they used Blastine, at a rate of six pounds per foot, and twenty feet of each hole was charged. To prevent a shell from igniting the charges, the four detonators for each charge were left out until shortly before detonation. All eight holes were scheduled to be blown two hours after Zero on 31 July, but the firing was delayed due to the advancing troops and wounded men.

III Bavarian Corps held the ground facing the Boesinghe sector. A week prior to the attack, British aviators reported that enemy trenches facing the Fifth Army front were manned at dawn but that the occupants withdrew during the day to avoid the severe bombardments. Following the German incursion into the British lines eight days earlier (14 July), the enemy front line troops had become increasingly anxious, fearing the eruption of apocalyptic mine explosions beneath their front line. Furthermore, the barrage caused one company of the 226th Reserve

Boesinghe bridge and the shell battered canal bank.

Infantry Regiment (49th Reserve Division) to retire without orders. Shortly after midnight on 25 July, a 2/Scots Guards raiding party on Baboon Trench (B6) confirmed that the bulk of the enemy had withdrawn. The valuable intelligence proved costly, for Lance Corporals Thom and Lyall were fatally wounded (they lie in Dulhallow ADS Cemetery VII E 14 and VII E 15), whilst eight others sustained wounds during the raid. As a matter of interest, unless already named, the British named enemy trenches in relation to their trench map reference letters, thus Baboon Trench, Baby Drive. The trenches in the adjoining grid began with a C, thus Cariboo, Caesar's Nose, etc.

During another patrol, two wounded men were left behind; Lieutenant Hambro and Private Smith of 3/Coldstream Guards volunteered to cross the canal. They recovered the men and also confirmed that the German forward defence system was unoccupied on the northern part of the Fifth Army front. This led Major General Fielding, commanding the Guards Division, to conceive an audacious plan for a daylight crossing of the canal, unannounced by an artillery bombardment. He immediately ordered Lieutenant Colonel Crawfurd, the commander of 3/Coldstream

Guards, to send out strong patrols, properly supported, to penetrate as far as Baboon Support Trench (B.6c and d), Artillery Wood and Cactus Junction.

At 5.20 pm on 27 July the patrols, supported by platoons and moppers-up, advanced and without much difficulty reached their objective. They overwhelmed the few Germans occupying the trenches so unobtrusively that the enemy in the rear trenches were unaware of the new tenants.

Royal Flying Corps observers also reported that the enemy had withdrawn from the front and second line of trenches facing the Royal Welsh Fusiliers. This proved to be untrue, as on hearing the approaching aircraft the Kaiser's men concealed themselves and restrained from firing at the low flying machine, leading the observer to assume the enemy had retired. When ordered to advance and reconnoitre, A Company 15/RWF reached the second line, only to be engaged by the enemy, who inflicted severe casualties on the outnumbered company. They sustained forty other ranks killed and the mortally wounded company commander, Major Evan Davies, was captured, along with a number of others; however, by the following day the Welsh Division held the east canal bank.

Private James William Lee, KinA 27 July 1917.

Other fatalities included Birkenhead man James William Lee, who had worked for twenty-three years at a local boot manufacturers prior to his enlistment 17 March

Wounded men lie in relative safety at an Aid Post near Boesinghe.

1915. Exactly one year later, 25705 Private Lee arrived in France. He left a wife and one child to mourn his loss, the thirty-four year old is commemorated on the Menin Gate. Private Edward Jones enlisted in May 1915, and, on completion of six months training, arrived on the Western Front. During the 27 July attack twenty-year old 54797 Private Jones was killed. His family still have a note, received in September 1917, from Corporal P Foulkes advising, 'You can rest content, he was buried decent, as I buried him myself'. The Mostyn soldier lies in Artillery Wood, X A 19.

235276 Private Douglas Anderton, 11 platoon, C Company, 15/RWF, wrote home:

Private E Jones is the Royal Welsh Fusilier standing on the right.

The featureless landscape is clearly shown in this photograph, taken near Boesinghe, of relaxed troops waiting further shell fire.

It is a terrible sight, the devastated country round here. You can look for miles and see nothing but one long stretch of shell-holes and battered trenches, not a tree nor a bush standing except a few jagged stumps, which look as if they have been struck by lightning. Bits of barbed wire, a heap of bricks that was once a farmhouse, some tangled ironwork once a railway, and a few tufts of scorched grass, and you have a picture of No Man's Land. The only living things are the rats and there are scores of them.

With the British now in possession of the east bank of the canal, 187th Tunnelling Company commenced boring holes in the canal bank, opposite the west bank tubes. These were charged with ammonal.

For two days 3/Coldstream remained unnoticed in their advance positions, quietly capturing a German patrol when it nonchalantly returned to its former trench. The episode was repeated on the 29th, when they captured an officer and his men, but others fled and raised the alarm. Soon low flying German aircraft came soaring over to investigate the situation and then German artillery bombarded the trenches unmercifully. The gains were held, thereby allowing the attack to start from the far bank and undoubtedly saved hundreds of lives.

The captured German line began near Bois Farm, on the fringes of Wood 14, and ran southeast, intersecting the Ypres-Staden railway,

Two bridges spanning the Yser canal in July 1917, the
nearest for infantry, the other for pack mules.

roughly 400 yards from the canal bank. To the extreme right of the line a protective flank was established, extending rearwards to the canal support trench. The French had also advanced and, along with 3 and 4/Coldstream Guards, established their new positions in the German first and support trenches, extending for 3,000 yards east and north of Boesinghe.

The Germans observed the allied offensive preparations from Pilckem Ridge. Allied Aircraft had largely neutralised the German advantage of prominent earthworks; instead, the myriad of shell holes provided innocuous cover for garrisons employed in the recent German strategy of 'defence in depth'. Machine-gun crews occupied tactically selected shell holes or concealed blockhouses that were incorporated into destroyed dwellings. Their low profiles made them difficult targets for artillery gunners. The posts, laid out in a chequer board pattern had overlapping field of fires, designed to break up the waves of troops, the survivors of which would stumble on into ever increasing resistance.

On the night of 29 July, a 1/Irish Guards patrol set off to examine a blockhouse (which later became known as pillboxes) and noted only small posts, held to the rear. Despite twice attracting fire, they returned with a prisoner, who said that 'the post held twenty men'. A small party, under Lieutenant Budd MC, kept the structure under observation. At daybreak six Germans, unable to fit into the overcrowded blockhouse, were seen sheltering in shell holes and sniped. This led to the surrender of the fourteen unwounded blockhouse occupants; the position was absorbed into the front line and held against the enemy's fire.

Low reinforced concrete blockhouse provides the backbone of German defence at Third Ypres. This example, with trench, was near Boesinghe.

Chapter Seven

PILCKEM RIDGE, THE FIRST PHASE OF THIRD YPRES

Throughout the fortnight prior to 31 July 1917, some 2,000 field guns along with 1,000 howitzers, heavy and medium calibre guns, hurtled over four million shells into the enemy lines. At Zero Hour, Thermite and flaming oil drums were added to the barrage, already of an intensity unequalled in the history of the war.

The front of the Allied attack extended from the Lys River opposite Deulemont, northwards to beyond Steenstraat, a distance of over fifteen miles. It aimed to seize the last stretch of significant front line ridges remaining in enemy hands in the sector after the victories of Vimy and Messines Ridges. The Fifth Army would strike the main blow on a seven and a half mile front, from the Zillebeke-Zandvoorde Road to Boesinghe inclusive. This chapter concentrates on the role of the Guards and 38th Divisions of XIV Corps. Second Army, positioned to the right of Fifth Army, initially played a secondary role by advancing only a short distance, forcing the enemy to distribute firepower over a wider area.

The objectives for the attacking waves in XIV Corps area were marked on maps as a series of coloured lines. The heavily shelled front line and support trenches were the Blue Line. Some 600 yards further on, the secondary German trenches, running across the Pilckem Road, were the Black Line. The third objective, or Green Line, was an imaginary line 100 yards beyond the well known Iron Cross-Kortekeer Cabaret Road,

A French photograph of the preliminary bombardment on the enemy lines east of the canal.

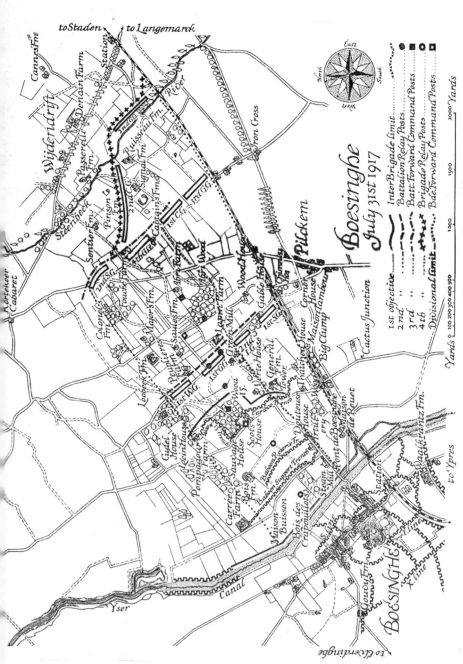

Sketch map showing the area of the Guards Division attack. The railway embankment seperated both divisions.

134

British artillery passing an old communication trench near Boesinghe 31, July 1917.

beyond Pilckem Ridge. The fourth objective, or Dotted Green Line, did not run parallel to the others, and though it crossed the Steenbeek on the right, this fourth line connected with the Green Line on the left. The anticipated distance of advance was just under two miles from the canal bank. In the north of the Salient the Guards Division and the 38th Division on their right would deliver the attack. The Ypres-Staden railway marked the limit between the British divisions, whilst to the left of the Guards stood the 1st French Division.

On a dark and misty 31 July morning, those with watches pensively watched the seconds tick away to Zero Hour. At precisely 3.50 am, the gun batteries roared into life with such intensity that they were reputed to have been heard on the south coast of England. The guns would provide a creeping barrage, incorporating forty-five pre-arranged lifts timed at four-minute intervals. This timetable allowed the infantry to advance at a rate of 100 yards closely behind its destructive onslaught.

Paul Maze, a French observer attached to General Gough, reported from the vicinity of Morteldje Estaminet:

...When the barrage finally opened, its violence was such that we looked at one another aghast... The wind caused by the displacement of the air was terrific – I might have been standing on the bridge of a ship during a typhoon and held on to the side of the

135

The old German line on the canal bank to the north of Boesinghe, captured by French troops.

trench like a weather rail. Gun-flashes were holing the sky as though thousands of signal lamp shutters were flashing messages... This bombardment exceeded anything I had witnessed before. The enemy retaliation was hardly noticeable. Suddenly I imagined I was seeing things when the top of our parapet seemed to move. But it was only the terrified rats fleeing in an army...

German infantry officer Georg Bucher wrote:

I went into my shelter and lay down fully dressed on my waterproof sheet. I fell into a doze, into forgetfulness... I could not have slept very long. The ground shook and resounded - a fierce bombardment was raging over Flanders, over the sector where we lay. My runner had already lit the candle when Sonderbeck burst into the dugout – he was the NCO on duty. "The big offensive has started!" he panted, his eyes rolling. I had never seen him in such a state of excitement. "Already three men have been blown to bits," he gasped and hastily swallowed a mouthful of rum. In a moment, I was ready and hurried up the steps with him. There was an absolute downpour of earth and shell splinters, on every side the night was lit up by explosions. Three of Sonderbeck's men were plastered on the walls of the trench or lying in fragments on the ground- the mess couldn't be cleared away while the bombardment lasted. I glanced at my wristwatch; it was time for Gaaten's spell of duty. I ran to his

shelter. Armed figures were standing in the flickering
candlelight.... "Time to go on duty!"
Five men followed Gaaten and me out of the dugout which, as things
were, was the only place of safety. Shells were exploding all around
us. The five silently took up their positions - they could only trust to
luck. There was a terrific explosion somewhere in the direction
from which we had just come- a hissing column of flame and earth
rose from the trench. Gaaten's dug out and the four men in it had
ceased to exist – a 15-inch shell had landed directly over it.

The Guards Division Attack

The leading battalions of 2 and 3 Guards Brigades were to capture the
Blue and Black lines, and the support battalions the Green Line. 1 Guards
Brigade would then pass through them and then seize the fourth line.

On the right of the division, Brigadier General Ponsonby's 2 Brigade
occupied the front from Boesinghe Bridge over the canal to the railway
bridge and would advance across difficult terrain, studded with strong
points. To their left, Seymour's 3 Brigade covered a larger frontage, 600
yards. The threatened rain held off and at 4.10 am, in order to comply
with the creeping barrage, two battalions from 2 Guards Brigade, 1/Scots
Guards and 2/Irish Guards, advanced in four waves, a hundred yards
apart. The sparsely held Blue Line offered little resistance and Cariboo
Trench, Wood 15 Trench and the large Wood 15, sited in the centre of
the German support trenches, were in the hands of the Guards by 4.30
am.

Meanwhile 1/Grenadier Guards and 1/Welsh Guards of Seymour's 3
Brigade, in position in Baboon Reserve Trench, approximately 500 yards
into enemy territory, waited for Ponsonby's Brigade to align with their
right. After biding their time, they advanced with the creeping barrage
and attained their first objective. When the leading companies came
under fire from two enemy blockhouses, Welsh Guardsman Sergeant
Robert James Bye rushed one of them and put it out of action, then
rejoined his company.

Both Guards' battalions suffered heavier casualties during their
successful assault on the Black Line. As the attacking troops progressed
to the Green Line, Bye volunteered to take charge of a party detailed to
clear up a line of blockhouses they had passed. He accomplished the task
and took many prisoners, taking still more when he afterwards advanced
to the Green Line. He displayed remarkable initiative throughout the
action and accounted for over seventy Germans. He became the first
Welsh Guardsman awarded the coveted Victoria Cross. The regiment had
been formed as recently as 26 February 1915 and initially consisted

Sergeant Robert Bye VC.

Welshmen who were encouraged to join from other Guards battalions.

After the consolidation of the new line, at zero plus three hours and twenty-four minutes, 4/Grenadiers and 2/Scots Guards passed through and attacked the Green Line. On their left flank, the 201st French Regiment encountered difficulties at Colonel's Farm, briefly stalling the advance, but, as the 2/Scots Guards swept past to the Green Line, the French captured the farm. Also on schedule, 2 Guards Brigade moved off towards the Black Line; however the Scots Guards suffered badly from fire from pillboxes on the railway and were forced to form a defensive flank and by the time they reached the Black Line their losses prevented an adequate defence of the front assigned to them. At 5 am 1/Coldstream, with 3/Grenadiers held in reserve some 400 yards from the canal, advanced, crossing the heavily shelled canal by means of damaged petrol can bridges.

They advanced in artillery formation towards Artillery Wood. When they reached the second line they found few British troops in front, owing

Construction sketch of an infantry petrol tin assault bridge.

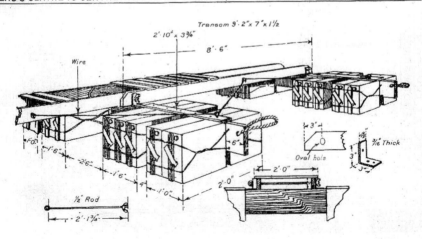

INFANTRY FOOT-BRIDGE.
PETROL TIN ASSAULT BRIDGE.
PIERS 8′ CENTRE TO CENTRE. WEIGHT OF PIER 110 LBS. WEIGHT OF TRENCH BOARD 48 LBS.

to the size of the Scots Guards casualties, indeed the battalion was still dealing with the pillboxes on their right. The murderous fire from machine-guns at Maison Tambour had already claimed twenty casualties from Number One Company. Captain W Neville (OC 3 Company, 3/Grenadier Guards) brought up Lewis guns, rifle and hand grenades and silenced the troublesome post.

The operations of 31 July resulted in the bestowal of twelve Victoria Crosses. Amongst the heroes was Private Thomas Whitham, 1/Coldstream Guards. During the advance, an enemy machine-gun began enfilading the battalion on his right. Private Whitham, acting on his own initiative, worked his way from shell hole to shell hole, passed through the creeping barrage and, when close enough, he rushed and captured the machine-gun, together with an officer and two other ranks.

Meanwhile the Scots Guards, released from guarding the right flank, in conjunction with 3/Grenadiers captured the Black Line, or second objective. Fire from the embankment pillboxes continued to create problems, whilst also delaying the advance of 38th (Welsh) Division.

Private Thomas Whitham VC, collecting his VC at Buckingham Palace.

A bunker and its occupants on Pilckem Ridge, 31 July 1917.

Several pillboxes on the left of 3/Grenadiers also blocked the advance Captain Eaton and others tackled these with Lewis guns and bombs, eliminating each obstacle. Number 1 Company surrounded a house, whose German occupants began frantically waving a white flag of surrender; three officers and fifty men became prisoners. While Captain Neville now had two machine guns in action beyond Wood House,

A Guards wiring party crosses the canal on a makeshift bridge of duckboards and stretchers, 31 July.

Numbers 1 and 2 Companies moved on and secured the Green Line. Captain Neville noticed that to the rear of his company, 38th (Welsh) Division, on the opposite side of the railway, were held up by three concrete blockhouses. Despite the risk of fire from the Welsh troops, Neville ordered an attack led by Sergeant Browning and Private Baker, both became wounded and yet took the position. In this action twenty Germans were killed and forty-two captured.

4/Grenadier Guards were to follow its Grenadier. When the Blue and Black lines were secured, the 4th Battalion would then pass through and take the Green Line. While crossing the canal they were heavily shelled and came under considerable machine gun fire coming from Crapouillot Wood. Understandably, two platoons became scattered, but Second Lieutenant Hubbard rallied the men. In the semi-darkness, the smaller Artillery Wood was mistaken for Wood 15 and at one period Irish, Scots and Grenadier Guards were mixed up south of Artillery Wood. The companies quickly separated and the advance continued by compass bearing, but a 5.9 shell landed amid the Battalion Forward Command Party, wounding many and creating great confusion. Lieutenant J B Burke, however, rapidly took command of the situation. On reaching the already captured Black Line, the 4th Battalion deployed in line to the left of 1/Coldstream. The 4th Battalion advanced; the water surrounding Lapin Farm briefly delayed Number 1 Company, but they caught up with the barrage before entering Abri Wood. All the pillboxes were rapidly surrounded and their occupants surrendered. Meanwhile, near Abri Farm, three trench mortars were captured, prior to the men reaching the Green Line, where they established a fortified line from Fourche Farm to Captain's Farm.

In accordance with the attack plan, Jeffrey's 1 Guards Brigade passed through the position, 2/Grenadiers taking up the right with 2/Coldstream to their left. The leading companies of 2/Grenadier Guards reached the Green Line and dug in on the crest of a hill, but suffered heavy casualties from machine gun fire from the right and enfilading fire from a ruined house east of the Ypres-Staden railway. The absence of the RWF on the right made the situation worse. Number 3 Company held the Green line, whilst the rest gallantly advanced to Signal and Ruisseau Farms, capturing a total of thirty German officers and men. Reinforcements arrived to bolster the front and the exposed right flank and Sergeant Sharpe and two men captured a blockhouse 150 yards west of the embankment, taking twenty-one prisoners.

By now the RWF had neutralised the blockhouses barring their advance, allowing Number 2 Company 2/Grenadier Guards to advance to within eighty-yards of the Steenbeek, where they established a position

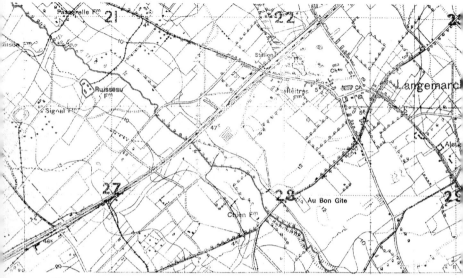

Trench map showing Ruisseau Farm, with the Steenbeek in close proximity.

with a good field of fire across the stream towards Langemarck.

The Guards had successfully penetrated almost two miles by 11 am; and all battalions were in touch with each other. The total casualties in the Guards Division during these operations amounted to fifty-nine officers and 1,876 men; 750 enemy were taken captive, along with thirty machine-guns and one howitzer. The French troops captured Steenstraat early in the day, pushed on and captured Bixschoote, along with the

Looking towards Langemarck from the junction of the embankment and the road leading to Ruisseau Farm, across which the Guards Division advanced on the final leg of the attack.

Happy to be alive – Grenadier Guardsmen seated amidst the ruins of a German machine gun position on Pilckem Ridge 31 July 1917.

German trenches to the south-east and west of the village, including Kortekeer Cabaret, which was the junction with the British troops. They had penetrated two miles over difficult terrain and had thereby secured the British flank.

The 38th (Welsh) Division attack

On the opposite side of the Ypres-Staden railway embankment, Major General C G Blackader's 38th (Welsh) Division were to capture the ruined village of Pilckem and a position on Pilckem Ridge midway between the Steenbeek and the village. Then two battalions of 115 Brigade would press on and capture the Steenbeek and its crossings.

Little remained of the hamlet of Pilckem but, amid the debris, lay concrete shelters resistant to heavy shells. Reports estimated that 280 pill-boxes were positioned in front of the division. Two days before the attack, fresh German troops from the Guards Fusiliers relieved the Pilckem defenders, taking up positions in three defensive lines. South of the hamlet, two trenches connected the advanced posts of Mackensen (C.8c.5.7), and Gallwitz Farm (C.8a.6.2), whilst another advanced

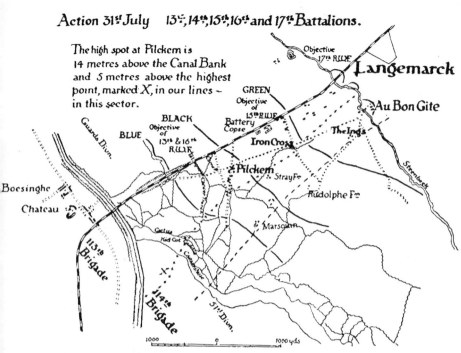

Action 31st July   13th, 14th, 15th, 16th and 17th Battalions.

The high spot at Pilckem is 14 metres above the Canal Bank and 5 metres above the highest point, marked X, in our lines – in this sector.

Sketch map from the Royal Welch Fusiliers history.

position, Zouave House, commanded the ground between both farms and the railway embankment.

On the eve of the 31 July attack, 13/RWF moved up to their assembly trenches: A and B Companies were in Harvey Trench (C.7.d. 8.5. 2 to C.7.c.8.5. 4.5); C Company were in Alma trench; while D were in Yorkshire Trench, where battalion headquarters occupied a deep dugout. The battalion frontage extended from C.7.d. 6.5. 6 to C.7.c.9.8, facing Caddie Trench. 14/RWF, assigned to carrying duties, moved up to their assembly trenches at B.24.b. 5. 9.5, close to Hulls Farm, prior to moving to Corridor Trench, between Bridge 6Z and Bridge 6W. Similar movements occurred across the divisional front; most of the bridges were wrecked but 6Z was still crossable. By 2.54 am on 31 July, all the attacking troops were in position east of the canal, 113 Brigade was disposed to the right of the railway embankment, 114 Brigade extended to their right and 115 Brigade was held in reserve.

> *The sight was one never to be forgotten. During the night, for six hours incessantly, the enemy batteries and lines were dealt with by gas shells, never for one moment did our shelling cease, and when the actual Zero hour came, boiling oil was poured on the enemy and the place became a perfect inferno, one of the outstanding features of the attack.* (1/Welsh Guards War Diary.)

At 3.50 am the whistles blew as members of 10 and 13/Welch Regiment together with the 13th and 16/RWF went over the top and advanced to their destiny. Their familiarity with the landmarks, learned on the Pilckem replica, proved to no avail, for darkness cloaked the battlefield. Guided by the creeping barrage, the attackers fell onto the Blue Line, carrying the objective with relative ease. By 5.20 am 13/RWF confirmed its capture, at the expense of only six wounded. Large numbers of prisoners, caught while sheltering from the barrage in dugouts in Caesar's Supports, were now shepherded to the rear. At Mackensen Farm (C8.c.), prisoners and a large store of ammunition, rockets, Very lights and trench mortars were captured.

As the first rays of sun appeared, the attackers encountered stiff resistance from their second objective, the Black Line. The centres of resistance were Marsouin Farm (C.8.b.) and Stray Farm (C.3.c.). East of Pilckem the 15/Welch advanced on the right centre, with 14/Welch on the right, across heavily entrenched terrain; but machine-gun emplacements were outflanked and their defenders, who offered no resistance, were taken prisoner.

East of the railway embankment 16/RWF's advance had stalled near Cancer Avenue Trench and Telegraph House (near Dragoon Camp cemetery). Some 500 yards east, a pillbox sited at Corner House cross roads curtailed the 13/RWF's advance and many brave men died attempting to rush the position. Corporal Davies, a former Welsh miner, who had previously served with the Royal Artillery, under cover of the artillery barrage raced forward and entered the pillbox. He bayoneted one of the machine-gun crew and brought in another man, together with a captured gun. The Fusiliers left the cover of shell holes and resumed the

Wounded at Boesinghe.

attack, only to come under withering fire from another weapon, concealed within Corner House. Corporal Davies, although wounded, then led a bombing party against the defended house, and eliminated the gun crew. The advance swept through the village, but in the process Corporal Davies suffered a second wound. By 6.00 am the Battalion held the Black Line. The advance to the final objective continued. As enemy bullets continually whittled down the Fusiliers, a sniper fatally drew the attention of James Davies. The twice-wounded corporal, who had refused medical attention, stalked the sniper; oblivious to the manoeuvring of the corporal the sniper continued to hold up the advance. Davies aimed and fired a single shot, silencing the sniper, and the advance moved on.

Corporal James Llewellyn Davies VC.

Davies, mortally wounded, died the next day; his widow collected his posthumously awarded Victoria Cross. Corporal James Llewellyn Davies's headstone in Canada Farm Cemetery (II B 18) bears the date 31 July 1917. The date is considered incorrect, as his platoon commander

Trench map showing the canal to Pilckem cross roads.

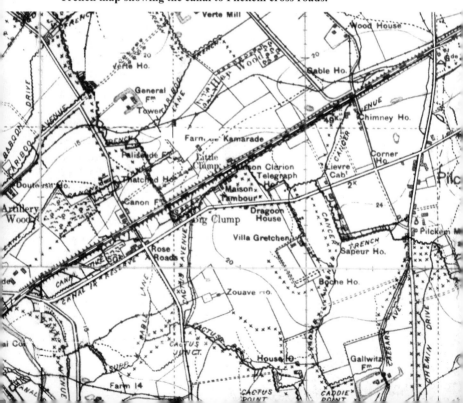

wrote to Mrs Elizabeth Davies advising her that her husband died of his wounds the day after his heroic actions.

Near Pilckem, 15/RWF struggled through a German barrage, sniper and machine-gun fire as they progressed to the Black Line. Now supported by six Lewis guns from 14/RWF and two companies of 16/RWF, they set off for the Green Line, only to encounter considerable resistance at Battery Copse and from houses in Brierley Road. About this time, the barrage left them behind, and the remaining officer, battalion commander Lieutenant Colonel C C Norman, ordered it to consolidate on Iron Cross Ridge. The battalion became the responsibility of RSM Jones, who consolidated the position 150 yards short of the Green Line.

235276 Private Douglas Anderton, 15th Royal Welsh Fusiliers wrote home later, saying

> *When we got to the third German line, I was just going into a dug out with my rifle levelled when two Fritzes came out, both armed. I just managed to pull the trigger on one and the other one threw up his hands. I took him prisoner and took his cap, belt, cig case and two or three souvenirs off him and shoved them in my haversack... We were held up by several machine guns but we bombed the Fritzs out of their concrete places and out they came shouting Kamerad...*

On the right of 15/RWF, the 14th and 15/Welch Regiment advanced, but came under fire from the direction of Rudolphe Farm (C3. d.), east of

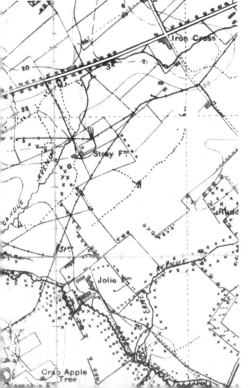

Pilckem, technically in the area allotted to the 51st Division, XVIII Corps. A 15/Welsh platoon successfully attacked the farm, taking fifteen prisoners whilst the rest of the garrison fled or were shot. The blood of the 14/Welch flowed freely during the assault on the Iron Cross area, but they rushed the defences, running twenty Germans through with the bayonet, took forty prisoners and also three machine guns. Moving on, they overran a dressing station, taking sixteen wounded and twenty-two others prisoners.

Finally, 14/RWF carried out sterling work carrying ammunition and water to all battalions. At about 6 pm Major W P Wheldon received orders for the battalion to advance at once. Due to 15/RWF not reaching the Green Line, the battalion was ordered to make two strong points on the Green Line, and dig a line of posts, to connect with 114 Brigade on the right and the Guards on the left. By 11.30 pm the strong points and post were finished.

11/SWB did not start their advance until 5.30 am (a hundred minutes after Zero Hour). The Battalion suffered only light casualties from shelling until 9.00 am, when the 11/SWB reached Iron Cross Ridge. Here they drew fire from machine gun posts and a farmhouse that the 51st Division had failed to reach. Machine guns in ruined houses or blockhouses continued to impede movement; one such weapon now opened fire on 11/SWB.

As the casualties increased, Sergeant Ivor Rees led his platoon forward by short rushes in an encircling sweep to the rear of the emplacement. Approximately twenty yards from the machine-gun, which was doing a great deal of damage, the sergeant rushed forward towards the gun team. He shot one, bayoneted another, then bombed the large concrete

Stretcher bearers in Pilckem village, 31 July, recovering from an exhausting days' work.

148

emplacement, killing five men, taking thirty prisoners, including two officers, and captured the undamaged weapon. Then he bombed the adjacent pillbox, killing five of its occupants whilst the remaining two officers and thirty men surrended; for his valour, Sergeant Rees was awarded the Victoria Cross.

During the fierce fighting for the ridge Captain Jenkins, commanding C Company, and the commander of D Company, Lieutenant Sayce, were wounded but 11/SWB and 17/RWF of 115 Brigade soon completed the capture of Iron Cross Ridge. They swept on towards the Steenbeek but they were now well behind the barrage and sustained many casualties from concealed machine-guns and

Sergeant Ivor Rees VC.

rifle fire. Held up by machine gun fire from the left, Second Lieutenant Vizer led his 11/SWB platoon against a machine gun, capturing the weapon, one officer and fifty prisoners, thereby allowing the advance to continue. The Steenbeek was crossed without much difficulty about 12.30 pm. The surviving attackers headed for the final objective, the Green Dotted Line, and within a few minutes A and C Companies reached Au Bon Gite. To their left were D Company, in sight of 17/RWF. In anticipation of an immediate counterstroke, consolidation work commenced straightaway, despite the bullets from snipers and machine guns from Langemarck, some 750 yards distant. About 3.00 pm two large enemy forces advanced from the Langemarck direction. 11/SWB's frantic calls for reinforcements were in vain, for the shelling severed the telephone cables; nonetheless they managed to hold their positions. However, 17/RWF were forced back across the Steenbeek and consequently the enemy won back their old concreted positions on 11/SWB's flank. This enabled the German machine guns to pour fire on the Au Bon Gite post, forcing the depleted South Wales Borderers to retire to the Steenbeek. Among the 11/SWB casualties was 18628 Sergeant Robert Blackwell of D Company, a veteran of two years' fighting, now posted as missing. Blackwell's chaplain later wrote to the bereaved mother:

I am sorry you have not been written to about your son. His platoon commander was killed and his company officer wounded, otherwise you would have heard. I regret that I cannot give you room to hope, but I think it will be wiser to tell you what actually occurred. His platoon went over the Steenbeek and were surrounded by the enemy, who intended to take them prisoner. Soon our men advanced, however, and the Germans retired. One can not say definitely that your son is a prisoner for the reason that others of his platoon came back and some say that your son was killed.

The name of Denbigh born Sergeant Robert Alun Blackwell is commemorated on Panel 22 of the Menin Gate Memorial.

10/SWB, held in reserve in Caddie Lane Trench (between Fortin 17 and Mackensen Farm), moved up, D Company arriving at 5 pm to reinforce their brother battalion. Meanwhile, three other companies dug a support line 300 yards in front of a road running south east (C.3. a, b

and d) from Iron Cross. The German 9th Grenadiers gathered in shell holes forward of Langemarck for a second counterattack. Their advance made little progress in the face of an artillery barrage and Lewis gun and rifle fire.

In the afternoon heavy rain fell, dissolving the pulverised ground into a sea of mud, and the mechanisms of rifles and Lewis guns jammed with it, requiring some of the 10/SWB Lewis guns to be returned to Battalion Headquarters at Rudolphe Farm for cleaning. This was the shape of things to come, for Third Ypres, better known as Passchendaele, became synonymous with a war waged in a quagmire.

German prisoners on Pilkem Ridge 31 July 1917.

As night fell on the successful opening day of the Third Battle of Ypres, this brief summary of the Boesinghe sector of the battle winds down. On 5 August 1917, 235276 Private Douglas Anderton, 15/RWF wrote home: *Dear Mother and Dad, I daresay you have seen in the papers about the big attack on July 31st, well I went over the top at dawn last Tuesday and today, Sunday, we have just come out of the line, all that is left of us, for a through rest. We went right through the three German lines and well beyond into open country, capturing the village of Pilckem on the way. When we could get no further, we dug a rough trench and had to hold our position against counter attacks night and day for five solid days. It was hell, especially when the rain started on the second day. The ground is very low and our trench was up to the waist in water all the time we held it, just in front of Langemarck.*

The Germans attacked us time after time, they shelled us, gassed us, bombed us and sniped us, but we held it like grim death until we were relieved yesterday. Our losses in this battalion are awful and there are only about 140 of us left out of a full battalion. We have had a lot of rain lately, and it makes all the difference here between 'comfort' and misery. It is not half so bad when you are dry even if 'Fritz' is strafing you, but when you are soaked through, and up over the knees in it into the bargain, it makes you feel rather tired of life.

Of the 630 prisoners the Welshmen took, over 500 were Guards Fusiliers nicknamed the 'Cockchafers'; the majority were from the 9th Grenadiers' and the 3rd Battalion of the Lehr Regiment, with a few from other units.

On day two of the battle, after a night of torrential rain, official photographer John Warwick Brook captured on film one of the most iconic images of the Great War, the trials of a quartet of stretcher-bearers as they stoically struggled through a morass of mud near Pilckem Ridge, with a laden stretcher, to a Boesinghe casualty clearing station.

After gaining the series of ridges east of Boesinghe, the British advance halted until 16 August, when the Battle of Langemarck commenced. During this uneasy lull in the fighting 173 Tunnelling Company meticulously surveyed the network of captured tunnels and thirty-five reinforced concrete dug outs. These varied in thickness from four to five feet thick, with parapets five feet high and four feet thick, formed from a series of wired together stakes, back filled with boards,

Stretcher-bearers 1 August 1917 heading for Boesinghe.

Taking a break from their labour in a scene of utter destruction, 5 August 1917, near Boesinghe.

British infantry crossing the canal at Boesinghe, 5 August 1917.

rubble and earth protecting their entrances. Their size and capacity, varied but the typical internal dimensions of these claustrophobic shelters were 5 x 5 x 4 feet and accommodated four men. These particular ones extended from north of Crapouillot Pontoon (the French boundary) to

south of the Boesinghe railway bridge. Linking the front line was a covered communication trench, which ran beneath the railway line to Canon Farm, near Artillery Wood.

The Royal Engineers also discovered a steep incline, excavated just north of the Boesinghe Road Bridge, which was an attempt to undermine its abutments. After twelve feet the incline ended abruptly, due to gravel and floodwater. Enemy attempts to destroy the neighbouring Boesinghe Railway Bridge also failed, despite excavating for over fifty feet underneath the embankment, when blue clay and water invasion defeated the tunnellers. The Sappers probed the clay walls with metal rods in a fruitless search for a hidden gallery, while keeping a wary eye on an unexploded German shell.

Another incline led to the South Mine (C.12.b.b5.4.5); beyond a depth of twenty feet the incline was completely wrecked but, undeterred British tunnellers cleared the rubble, until at forty two feet they reached a level chamber. About thirty feet down the enemy had created a small chamber and filled it with "rum jars" (projectiles for a timber trench mortar reinforced with steel bands). German sappers exploded the "rum jars" to

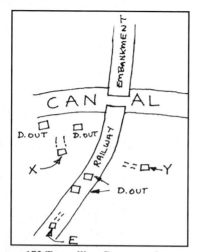

173 Tunnelling Company dug out reconnaissance sketch. After pumping dry the gallery marked 'E' the RE discovered 1,800 lbs of perdite and ammoniate salts which they destroyed.

create a spherical cavity a few feet across, housed a windlass, with a steel rope for hauling spoil, a slide and a fan with assorted piping. Below was a deep sump filled with water, pumped from below. On the right of the chamber ran a sixty-two feet long gallery, containing a pump for lifting the water from the sump to the surface. The gallery, constructed between May and July, led half way to the railway, but ended in a face of blue clay. Canal water leaked into the workings and, arguably, this caused the abandonment of the second attempt to undermine the abutments.

Above the battlefields the Royal Flying Corps became the eyes of the Royal Artillery, spotting falling shells and locating enemy batteries, while striving to protect the British lines from marauding hostile aircraft. On 6 September a routine patrol by 20

A Royal Engineers sketch of the mine positions.

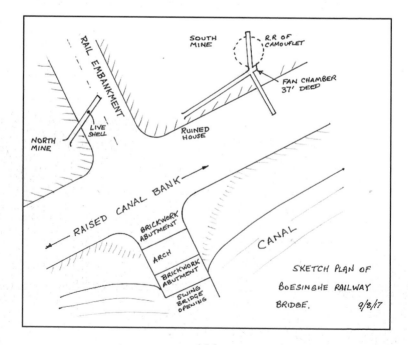

17 August 1917. Men take cover from the shells attempting to destroy a camouflaged 8-inch howitzer, sited near Boesinghe.

Men struggle through the mud near Boesinghe in August 1917. They are encumbered by their waterproof capes as they carry a timber section of a bridge to the Yser canal.

Muscle power – human and animal – were essential in the war. Hauling a six-inch howitzer through Boesinghe, 16 August 1917.

Leutnant **Werner Voss**

Squadron took off from Ste-Marie Cappel aerodrome and set a course for the Salient. Amongst the flight was an Fe 2d, piloted by twenty-five year old Lieutenant John Oscar Pilkington, accompanied by his observer, 1712 Second Class Airman Herbert Frederick Mathews. Over Boesinghe the British encountered a hostile patrol of *Jasta* 10, comprising five Albatross Scouts and a Fokker F1 tri plane, the later flown by Lieutenant Werner Voss, who had already registered forty-one kills (Voss downed forty-eight aircraft before his death in an epic engagement on 23 September 1917).

During the ensuing dogfight, Lieutenant Pilkington engaged an Albatross Scout, which fell to the ground in a tight spiral. According to Voss it was 3.35 pm (German time) when his triplane locked onto the tail of Pilkington's Fe 2d B1895. After several machine gun bursts, the British fighter burst into flames and neither aviator survived. Lieutenant J O Pilkington is buried in Bailleul

Communal Cemetery Extension III E 202; his twenty-two year old observer occupies the next grave.

As the individual battles of Third Ypres raged across the ridges, Boesinghe became a hive of activity as troops slogged up to the line, or grim faced, mud encrusted survivors trailed through, grateful to have survived engagements waged in a swamp. Amongst the incoming units was 1/6 DLI, who arrived at Hulls Farm camp on 26 October, only to find the camp still occupied by 4/Northumberland Fusiliers, scheduled to move up that afternoon to participate in an attack along the Ypres-Staden railway, north of Poelcapelle. While the Durhams waited in a field, a squadron of German Gotha bombers soared overhead. A stick of bombs erupted in the midst of the Durhams; of the score of casualties, eight other

10 September 1917. Two ambulances in Boesinghe ready to transport wounded men to the rear. Several veterans noted how excruciatingly painful each journey could be as the vehicles bumped over the damaged roads.

A busy scene during the Third Battle of Passchendaele: prisoners are being escorted in and troops are moving up. The dead horse is ignored by almost everyone.

ranks died immediately and probably two others succumbed to their wounds before the end of the month. The Tyne Cot memorial bears the names of six of the Gotha victims.

The offensive in this area that had begun so promisingly developed into a series of protracted engagements that became collectively known as the

A German Gotha bomber.

Battle of Passchendaele. For further information, the reader should consult a specialist book on this evocative subject, a fine example being Battleground *Ypres - Passchendaele* by Nigel Cave.

British soldiers leaving billets in a badly shelled village near Boesinghe, in 1918.

EPILOGUE

A spring of devastating reversals

The war of attrition drained the opposing armies of manpower. However, after Russia's collapse in late 1917 German troops no longer required on the Eastern Front were transferred to the Western Front at a time when British reinforcements were restricted. While the Allies appeared content to wait for sufficient American troops to tip the numerical balance in their favour, Germany prepared for a spring offensive.

The expected storm broke in the Somme region on 21 March, when Ludendorff launched his carefully planned Spring Offensive across a sixty mile stretch of the Western Front. The blows struck at the junction of the French and British armies. Within a fortnight the enemy had penetrated up to forty miles. The attack ground to a halt on 5 April; but four days later a secondary attack broke out in Flanders. 'Operation Georgette' struck the Ypres to La Bassee areas, recapturing in hours objectives that the allies had, seemingly, taken an eternity to capture.

Within the Salient the first stage of a withdrawal commenced on the night of 12/13 April, so that only outposts now defended Passchendaele Ridge. The withdrawal went a stage further three nights later, when British troops withdrew to the Steenbeek and the Westhoek and Wytschaete Ridges. Battle hardened men must have wept as they abandoned ground steeped in the blood of so many fallen comrades.

Boesinghe April 1918.

Douglas Haig wrote:

> *On 16 April, the enemy launched a strong assault upon the right of the Belgian Army about the Ypres-Staden railway. This attack, the object of which was to capture Bixschoote and advance beyond the Yser canal, ended in complete failure. The capture of Kemmel Hill seriously threatened our positions in the salient.... A further re-adjustment of our line in the salient was accordingly carried out on the night of 26/27 April, our troops withdrawing to the general line Pilckem – Wieltje – west end of Zillebeke Lake – Voormezeele.*

The next day the enemy launched another attack upon the Ypres-Staden railway. Determined counter-attacks by the Belgians ejected the German infantry from ground held since their previous assault. Throughout these days of crisis, despite the enemy gaining the west canal bank, the Belgians denied them Boesinghe (and other objectives). The wrecked village resumed its familiar frontline role until late September 1918. The Allies then began the advance which finally ended the horror of the war of attrition that had dragged on for well over four years.

162

TOUR ONE

A Walking Tour of Essex Farm and area
(sixty to ninety minutes duration)

From Poperinghe take the N38 until the turn off for the N369, then head towards Boesinghe. If you are travelling from Ypres, head north along the N369, this will take you beneath the N38 flyover; travellers from the direction of Poperinghe join the N369 about here. A few hundred yards beyond the flyover, on your right, is Essex Farm cemetery. Park in the lay-by. Take care, for the N369 traffic moves deceptively quick.

Essex Farm in the late 1920s.

Essex Farm Cemetery is one of the most frequently visited cemeteries in the Salient, due to its association with the renowned poem *In Flanders Fields*, and the nearby fine example of a restored Advanced Dressing Station. The name of Essex Farm probably refers to a roadside cottage formerly located at the junction of the canal path and highway. Precisely who first coined the phrase 'Essex Farm' is lost in the mists of time; however, the name is attributed to members of 2/Essex, a component of the 4th Division that arrived here in the summer of 1915.

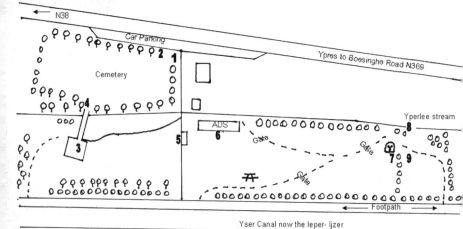

1. The Cross of Sacrifice.   2. Albertina Memorial.   3. 49th Division Memorial.   4. Stone of Sacrifice.   5. The John McCrae Memorial.   6. Advanced Dressing Station.   7. Canal bank bunker.   8. Footbridge.   9. RE Field Company Orderly Room bunker

On the grass verge, close to the Cross of Sacrifice (**1**), stands one of the two dozen white Albertina Memorials (**2**) placed by the Belgians at important Great War sites. This particular one was unveiled in November 1985 to commemorate the writing here of *In Flanders Fields*. The memorial differs from all the others, as it has an engraved poppy.

There are 1,099 Great War soldiers buried or commemorated within Essex Farm cemetery, with another 102 headstones marking the graves of unidentified soldiers 'Known unto God'. Special memorials also record nineteen soldiers whose graves were lost, probably due to shellfire, but are believed to be buried here. Within Plot 1 are some of the 1915 fatalities of the 49th (West Riding) Division. Throughout the autumn of 1916 the dead of the 38th (Welsh) Division steadily filled up Plot 3. The remaining graves, including five graves of prisoners, are in no particular order.

Albertina Memorial and the Cross of Sacrifice, Essex Farm Cemetery.

In Plot 1 Row U Grave 8 a small forest of poppies draws attention to the grave of an under age soldier. His death was recorded in the 22 January 1916 edition of the *Dorking and Leatherhead Advertiser*:

164

... Private Valentine Joe Strudwick, of the 8/Rifle Brigade, joined up twelve months ago last January. At the time of his death, on 14 January, he had not reached his sixteenth birthday, having been born on Valentine's Day (hence his name) *1900. His mother would naturally have liked to have kept him out of the army for a year or two, but young Strudwick would have none of it... With only six weeks of training, the lad was sent over to France. Within a short time, he lost two of his chums who were standing near him, both instantaneously killed. The shock was such, with the addition of being badly gassed, that he was sent home and was for three months in hospital at Sheerness. On recovery, he joined his regiment in France and this week his mother received the following letter dated 15 January.*

'I am very sorry indeed to have to inform you that your son was killed by a shell on 14 January. His death was quite instantaneous and painless and his body was carried by his comrades to a little cemetery behind the lines, where it was reverently buried this morning. A cross is being made and will shortly be erected on his grave.'

Rifleman V J Strudwick's headstone.

Rifleman Strudwick was not the youngest to die in the Salient. It is believed that Private John Condon, 2/Royal Irish Rifles, was a year younger; he rests in Poelcapelle British Cemetery.

An observant visitor may notice the Victoria Cross engraved on the headstone of Private Thomas Barratt VC (sometimes spelt Barrett), who is interred in Plot 1 Row Z Grave 8. Thomas was born on 5 May 1895 in Dudley, Worcestershire. After his mother died, the six-year old was raised in the workhouse. He later resided at Dark House Lane Coseley and gained employment in a local engineering works. In January 1915, the twenty year old enlisted in the South Staffordshire regiment, where 17114 Private Barratt rapidly established a reputation as a tenacious individual. The 7/South Staffordshire served in Gallipoli and Egypt prior to arriving on the Somme in July 1916. The following July, ahead of Forward Cottage (C.21.b), the soldier stalked and killed enemy snipers but, after returning safely to the British lines, he was killed by a shell. He received a posthumous award of the Victoria Cross, gazetted 6 September 1917.

Private T Barratt VC and headstone.

Private I Hanington Murray.

Second Lieutenant R A M Lutener

Plot 1 also contains the graves of five Canadians who were probably victims of the early gas attacks. The headstone of Private Ivor Hanington Murray (Plot 1 Row L grave 2) records his death as being between 23rd and 30 April; however Veterans Affairs Canada give 23 April, and he has the dubious distinction of being the earliest recorded death in this cemetery. Several other Canadians soon joined him and the cemetery developed around these interments.

Some of the lesser known names engraved on the headstones will be familiar to the reader. Plot 1 Row B Grave 4 contains Second Lieutenant R A M Lutener 6/KSLI, the fourth sniper victim in twenty minutes. Another KSLI officer, Alec Leith Johnston, who wrote for *Punch* magazine, rests in Plot 1 Row Q Grave 19. Also in this plot, in Row D Grave 19 is Private B Wright, who was killed by a shell while sitting on a firestep, immersed in waist deep water. Grouped by the steps to the War Stone are members of 2/Irish Guards, killed during an unsuccessful 2 July 1917 raid to locate gas engines. On 12 June 1917 a 5.9 shell exploded into a canal bank dugout occupied by 39 Divisional Signal Company RE. The casualties were three dead, two fatally wounded and one less seriously. The eighteen and nineteen years old Sappers Imison, Pereira and Leggett are buried alongside each other in Plot 2, U 1, 2 and 3 respectively.

On the canal bank to the rear of the cemetery stands a tall obelisk constructed from Belgian granite. This is the 49th (West Riding) Division Memorial (**3**), designed by architects Brierly and Rutherford, 13 Lendal, York. The Imperial War Graves Commission (The 'Imperial' was later replaced by 'Commonwealth') had by July 1920 an architect's plan for the cemetery. Sir Reginald Blomfield, who was one of the leading CWGC architects, considered that the memorials proposed location allowed the obelisk to dominate the cemetery. Believing access through Essex Farm Cemetery would interfere with his design, he suggested access to the memorial should be along the canal bank, or the memorial should be incorporated within the cemetery or, ideally, located elsewhere, opposite the west corner of the cemetery being one of the options. The debate continued until March 1923, when Blomfield reached an agreement to position the obelisk and access bridge (**3**) (over the Yperlee) directly behind the Stone of Sacrifice (**4**). The cemetery was completed in 1925.

Interestingly, the (possibly original) cemetery plans on the CWGC website show a pronounced boundary between the cemetery and memorial. It may be coincidental that the Cross of Sacrifice stands in the centre of the cemetery entrance, on an axis that hides the canal bank obelisk. The position is also as far away as possible from the divisional memorial so disliked by the cemetery architect.

The 49th (West Riding) Division Memorial was unveiled on 22 June 1924 by Major General Edward Maxwell Perceval CB DSO, who commanded the division from July 1915 to October 1917. Over the intervening years the cemetery saplings have matured, allowing nature to lessen the impact of the once very conspicuous memorial.

The 49th (West Riding) Division memorial.

Now make your way back to the cemetery entrance and take the path that leads to the Yser canal. On your left, you will see the John McCrae Memorial (**5**). This is a Historical Sites and Monuments Board of Canada Memorial, officially unveiled on Saturday 29 October 2005. A large, bronze, multi-lingual plaque summarises John McCrae's (1872-1918) career and an adjoining plaque bears McCrae's poem. Incorporated into the memorial is a CWGC style locker

The inauguration of the 49th Division memorial, which took place in June 1924.

The John McCrae memorial.

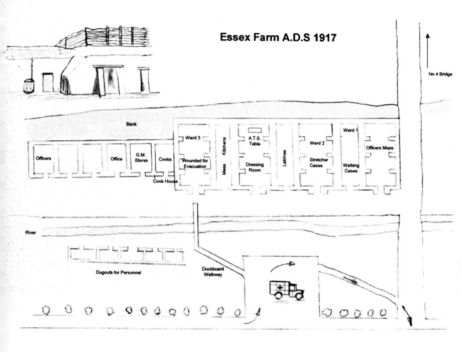

The layout of the 1917 ADS at Essex Farm.

containing the Memorial Register.

To the left of the memorial, set into the earth bank, is a long concrete bunker, possibly built on the site of the original timber and elephant iron dressing station in existence during Second Ypres. At the far end of the bunker pathway is an information notice. The existing concrete Essex Farm Advanced Dressing Station (ADS) (**6**) was constructed in 1916, after McCrae had departed.

The cramped confines of the inner compartments, coupled with its buttress walls, increased the integral strength of the structure. A protective bank of earth shielded one elevation and extended over the ADS roof. A protective wall of sandbags shielded the ADS front walls, making the structure impervious to all but a direct hit. The front line wounded arrived over the nearby Number Four (Brielen) Bridge; the more seriously wounded were evacuated by motor ambulances stationed in front of the ADS, whilst the less fortunate lie in the adjacent cemetery.

After falling into disrepair, the ADS, after extensive restoration, officially re-opened on 3 May 1995, the eightieth anniversary of McCrae writing his immortal poem.

Essex Farm ADS while is use by the army.

After falling into disrepair, the restored ADS is again comfortably accessible to the public.

In Flanders fields the poppies blow
Between the crosses, row on row
That mark our place; and in the sky
The larks, still bravely singing, fly
Scarce heard amid the guns below.
We are the dead. Short days ago
We lived, felt dawn, saw sunset glow,
Loved and were loved, and now we lie
In Flanders fields.
Take up your quarrel with the foe:
To you from failing hands we throw
The torch; be yours to hold it high.
If ye break faith with us who die
We shall not sleep, though poppies grow
In Flanders fields.

John McCrae 1915.

The poppy became an enduring symbol of remembrance following its first use by the fledgling Haig Fund (Poppy Appeal) on Armistice Day 1921. Lieutenant Helmer, whose death inspired the poem, is

commemorated on the Menin Gate, for his grave was lost during the war years. John McCrae suffered with asthma, a condition aggravated by exposure to poison gas. Weakened by the mental and physical strain of his occupation, McCrae contracted pneumonia. The forty-five year old Lieutenant Colonel McCrae died on 28 January 1918 and is buried in Wimereaux Command Cemetery, IV H 3, near Boulogne.

Retrace your steps, walk past the McCrae Memorial and follow the short path leading to the canal bank. Number Four (Brielen) Bridge spanned the canal here by the modern Kanaal Ieper-Ijer sign. Edmund Blunden wrote

The most solid bridge, Number 4, was a ferocious target; but at the Ypres end, called the Dead End, the new causeway was swollen with dead mules, pushed out of the road on to the sloping bank. The water below, foul yellow and brown, was strewn with full-sized eels, bream and jack, seething and bulged in death. Gases of several kinds oozed from the crumbled banks and shapeless ditches, souring the air.

North of the bridge the British erected their first dummy or 'Sham Tree' for observing the enemy. This was the idea of Solomon Joseph Solomon, a distinguished Pre-Raphaelite artist and member of the Royal Academy,

A contemporary sketch of the ADS.

commissioned as a colonel in one of the Royal Engineers' camouflage units. Detailed sketches and measurements were taken of a canal bank tree and a replica was fabricated from steel tubular sections, clad externally with bark from a decayed Windsor Park willow. The tree weighed over seven hundredweight and required a dozen men to lift it. During the hours of dark, sappers cut down the original canal bank tree and substituted it with the replica. On entering through a trench, an observer could climb an internal ladder within the tree and direct artillery undetected through a loophole. A painting by Colonel Solomon, depicting the erection of this tree, is in the

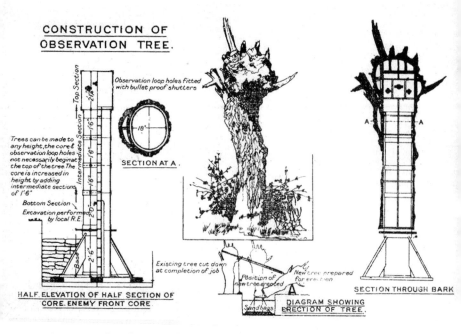

CONSTRUCTION OF OBSERVATION TREE.

Top Section

Intermediate Section

Observation loop holes fitted with bullet proof shutters

Trees can be made to any height, the core & observation loop holes not necessarily begin at the top of the tree. The core is increased in height by adding intermediate sections of 1'6"

Bottom Section

Excavation performed by local R.E.

Base

HALF ELEVATION OF HALF SECTION OF CORE. ENEMY FRONT CORE

SECTION AT A.

Existing tree cut down at completion of job

Position of new tree erected

New tree prepared for erection

Sandbags

DIAGRAM SHOWING ERECTION OF TREE.

A——A

SECTION THROUGH BARK

A construction diagram of an observation tree.

A bunker that was once embedded into the canal bank.

After the Armistice homeless civilians used the bunkers as accommodation.

Imperial War Museum, a lasting reminder of the forty-five such trees erected on the Western Front.

   To the right of the footpath is another John McCrae site information board. On the opposite corner is a small cycle stand; take the grass path leading up the bank, originally created in the seventeenth century, under the direction of the French military architect Vauban. This fortification,

A footbridge made from light railway track.

for over half a century, marked the northern border of Louis XIV's French empire. Over 450 yards of this site is now accessible to the public. Walk towards the picnic bench, past two interesting site information boards, and through the gate. This is where batteries of the 1st Canadian Artillery Brigade stood during Second Ypres.

Follow the well-trodden grass path over the bank, and head over to your left to another wooden gate. Below, a few steps and a duckboard path are visible going past a Canal Bank Bunker (**7**). Only the arched concrete front and low walls, containing an elephant iron roof panel, have survived. However, this is a good example of one of the many bunkers in existence here during the war. After the Armistice such bunkers became temporary homes to the returning people.

A few feet behind you runs the Yperlee stream. Alongside the modern concrete wall you will see a narrow footbridge constructed from light railway track. (**8**)

A few yards past the bridge, is a circular manhole; to the right of this, a low concrete wall protrudes from the canal bank; this is another bunker. An engraved slab embedded into the bunker side says that this was a RE Field Company Orderly Room. (**9**) (If you anticipate problems walking this latter section there is an easier access. Approximately 300 yards on your right from the cemetery entrance, the white wall is visible from the N369. Park and walk towards the wall.)

Now retrace your steps towards the canal bank. Follow the right hand fork in the grass path, and this will lead you back to the cobbled path running alongside the ADS. Return to your vehicle and head towards Boesinghe.

A barely noticeable RE Field Company Orderly Room bunker protrudes from the canal bank.

Close up of the bunker identification.

TOUR TWO

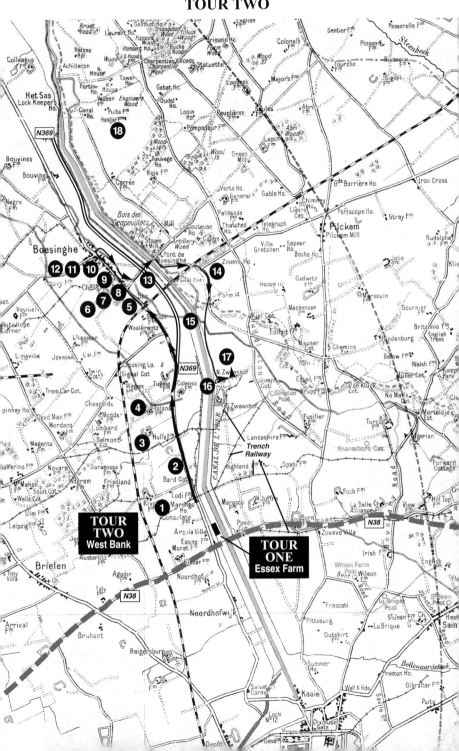

TOUR TWO

West bank (car tour) of approximately two hours

When following Tour Map Two the tour circuit distance is approximately four miles

A couple of hundred yards further north, on the left hand side of the road, a light railway snaked its way from Austerlitz Farm, east of Brielen. Near Marengo House (**1**), the track split in two directions. One track followed the Boesinghe road, the other ran across Number Six Bridge, where a spur ran to Glimpse Cottage. The main track continued past Spahi Farm, before terminating at Turco Farm. About 500 yards, from Essex Farm pull in near the red brick porticos of Bard Cottage Cemetery (**2**) **Start here.**

The name of this cemetery derived from a house near to a bridge named Bard's Causeway. The site benefited from a high bank, which concealed all local activity. The earlier mentioned light railway track ran between the cemetery and the road. As the rolling stock conveyed men and supplies to and from the front, it would seem logical to use the same method to move corpses to this and other cemeteries. The burials here began in June 1915, continuing until October 1918, when cemeteries more convenient for the advanced front line were established. The 49th (West Riding) and 38th (Welsh) Divisions are well represented here. Other headstones stand testimony to a cornucopia of units who defended this part of the Salient, including the men who 'fed the guns' during the autumn advance of 1917.

Lieutenant Slingsby, killed while laying a telephone wire.

Today there are 1,639 men buried or commemorated here, thirty-nine of whom are unidentified, and three lost graves are recorded on special memorials. Each headstone marks a tragic end of life and a flood of loved ones tears. Here you will find in Plot 2 B16 to B19 the Liverpool Scottish men killed whilst minding the line during the absence of a large Royal Welsh Fusilier raiding party. Casualties from the raid conducted near Essen Farm are also here, including Acting Captain Ormsby, who died of wounds after the 18 February 1917 raid; four of his party are in graves Plot 2 C14, 15, 16 and 19.

Lieutenant Slingsby, shot dead while laying a telephone line, is also here. The sad epitaph on the headstone of Second Lieutenant Walter Behrens, C

Bard Cottage Cemetery in the early twenties.

The cemetery today, viewed from a slightly different angle.

Battery 122 Brigade RFA, explains his demise; 'Killed near front line while searching for wounded comrades'.

Brigadier-General Hull of Hull's Farm fame led the first counter attack against the Germans at St Julien.

Near the rear of the cemetery, in Plot 5, Row A, are six graves of men from 55 Company Machine Gun Corps, killed on 10 October 1917. The men were ordered forward to defend a crossroads bombarded by the enemy. As the pack mules bringing up their weapons were delayed by the poor ground, the men took cover until they arrived. When the machine gunners broke cover to unload their equipment, a shell erupted in their midst, killing eight men and wounding fourteen more. The survivors relieved 32 Company MGC near Poelcapelle church.

In Plot 4, Row C, you will see forty-six graves brought here after the Armistice; some were isolated graves, but thirty-two were originally in the nearby Marengo Farm Cemetery. They were June 1915 casualties from 1/East Lancashire and 2/Seaforth Highlanders. The French troops based in the farm prior to the British occupancy of this sector gave the farm its name. The cemetery was sited a few hundred yards to the south of Bard Cottage and was used from June 1915 until August 1916.

Return to your vehicle and continue towards Boesinghe, on your left, set back from the road, is **Hull's Farm**, apparently named after Brigadier-General Hull, a Brigade Staff Officer here in April 1915 (**3**). Another light railway crossed the road approximately 250 yards before the farm access road. The track crossed the canal, terminating at North Zwaanhof Farm and extended in an arc rearwards, connecting Elverdinghe and to beyond Lizerne.

On the opposite canal bank is the industrial zone, which covers a large area of the old battlefield. During my brief visit in April 2009, two large wind turbines were erected, there now may be more. The turbines are prominent from most parts of the battlefield and are a useful landmark. Roughly one mile from Essex Farm you will see a green CWGC sign, pull in on the right alongside a modern looking house. Cross the road, to **Talana Farm Cemetery** (**4**) accessed by a 300 yard grass pathway.

The military decided to name a group of farmhouses here after battle locations of the South African War, consequently on contemporary maps

Talana Farm Cemetery, Boesinghe.

such names as Tugela Farm, Colenso Farm, Belmont Farm and Talana Farm can be found. French Zouaves began this cemetery during April 1915. After the arrival of the 4th Division in the area, 1/Rifle Brigade and 1/Somerset Light Infantry buried their dead here, followed by other units until March 1918.

A total of 529 First World War servicemen are buried or commemorated here, of whom fourteen are unidentified. Special memorials honour six casualties believed to be in the cemetery whose graves were lost, possibly due to shellfire. The site was approximately three-quarters of a mile behind the British front line and within range of most artillery. 9/Rifle Brigade erected a now long gone wooden cross here, commemorating their comrades who fell in January and February 1916.

Men killed in the successful attack on International Trench are well represented here; for eighty-four of the headstones bear the date 6 July 1915. These men are located in the two longest rows of graves, Plot 2 Row E and F. An officer wrote to the Burnley family of one of them, 6184 Private James McCarthy 1/East Lancashire:

> ... he was killed yesterday morning on Tuesday 6 July. ...I was holding a trench with (censored) men and there was a heavy bombardment all day yesterday. Two shells dropped into the trench and killed eight men of my platoon. James was amongst them. Most of them were old hands and have done duty here since the start and they will be a great loss to me...

McCarthy was a veteran of the South African war; it seems ironic he

179

Headstone of Private Henry Stanworth, who implored the shirkers to enlist.

survived that conflict, only to be killed sixteen-years later and be buried (II E 35) in a cemetery probably named after the Battle of Talana Hill.

7349 Private Henry Stanworth, 1/East Lancashire, was a professional cornet player and a pre war territorial soldier. Due to a year long contract in Wales, he missed the mobilisation of his unit, but at the first opportunity joined the East Lancashire Regiment. While at Plymouth he declined a position in the band in preference to going to the front with the Regulars. In the trenches, the Burnley soldier penned six verses of poetry aimed at the shirkers back home. One verse read:

Come, brothers, come, just think,
And don't like cowards from the enemy shrink,
Just think what depends upon this war,
And think of us from home so far.

Private Stanworth was killed by a shell on 6 July (II F 24). Among the many victims to snipers are three men from 1/6 Duke of Wellingtons, interred here in late 1915. A bullet through the left eye killed Private John Baxter (III F 7). Private Albert Toon while in F31 sustained a bullet to the head (IV D 7), as did Private E Thompson (IV D 10) while in F34.

Return to your vehicle and drive north towards Boesinghe, passing on

The pulverised station was re-built after the war. The station building still exist but the rail track is long gone.

your right the site where Colenso Farm stood. Approaching on your left is Tugela Farm. If you look towards the industrial zone, this point is roughly where the light railway, shielded by the canal bank, terminated. You are now about 800 yards from the front line and getting closer. Continue; you will see a blue sign for Boesinghe, and 800 yards from the cemetery turn left into Diksmuideweg, a side road on the outskirts of Boesinghe. Now a side road this was once a main road until the construction of the N369 which bypasses the village.

Go slowly through the modern part of Boesinghe village, three-quarters of a mile from the last cemetery, there is a small hump in the road, to the left is the rebuilt but now redundant Boesinghe Station (**5**).

Continue for approximately 200 yards, and on your left, next to a blue road sign, there is a Demarcation Stone (**6**) marking the limit of the Spring 1918 German advance.

In the decade after the Armistice, the Touring Club de France, in conjunction with the Touring Club de Belgique and the Belgian Government, commissioned Demarcation Stones. The sculptor, Paul Moreau Vauthier, designed three variations to the memorials, the most notable difference being the pattern of the helmet. The helmet and legend 'Here the invader was brought to a halt' reflected the nationality of the troops holding the line at each location, though this was a far from exact procedure.

A demarcation stone marking the approximate limit of the German advance.

In the adjoining private garden there is an ivy clad observation bunker (**7**) that once had an unrestricted view of the canal bank. Mounted on the bunker roof is *Kleine Berta* (**8**), a well maintained German *Minnenwerfer* trench mortar.

German trench mortar mounted on a roadside observation bunker.

Further along is woodland bounded by the tall railings of Boesinghe Chateau (**9**). The ruins served as a brigade headquarters, and field ambulances established ADS here. This is private property but it is possible to glimpse the rear of the chateau, whose grounds once contained the graves of nineteen soldiers,

The original grave of Lance Corporal J Lyall.

principally from the Guards Division, who were killed or died in June 1917. One such grave belonged to 15749 Lance Corporal James Lyall, who died on 25 June 1917; he now rests in Dulhallow ADS Cemetery VII E 15.

A few hundred yards further along the road is Boesinghe Church (**10**) (Sint-Michaels Kirk), and a CWGC sign pointing up a narrow path. Walk a few yards up the path, working your way around the left of the church. Heading for a calvary, to the right are fourteen CWGC headstones (**11**). With the exception of one grave, these are Second World War graves, the result of the defence of Belgium and the 1940 withdrawal to Dunkirk.

The headstone (1 A 1), standing slightly forward of the others, belongs to Captain Edward Frederick Maltby Urquhart of 1/Black Watch (Royal Highlanders), who was killed on 23

The CWGC Boesinghe churchyard. The far left grave is the only Great War grave.

October 1914, near Kortekeer Cabaret. On hearing rumours of another officer's interment within the churchyard, the author contacted the CWGC, who confirmed that they had transferred the grave of Lieutenant Bowes-Lyon elsewhere.

Both officers were killed on the same day and, after their funeral, a temporary wooden cross marked each grave. The heavy shelling destroyed the churchyard and an initial search for the officers remains' was unsuccessful and the graves were feared lost. During the post Armistice restoration of the cemetery, however the remains of both officers were found. In compliance with the wishes of the Urquhart family, their relation was re-interred within the cemetery, along with the recovered fellow officer. However, the Bowes-Lyon family had previously stipulated that if the remains were found, they preferred an interment in a British cemetery. On realising the error, Lieutenant Bowes Lyon was again exhumed, and is buried in New Irish Farm Cemetery XXX D 11.

Captain Edward F M Urquhart.

Retrace your route back to the road, turn left and on the corner facing a car park is a Belgian war memorial (**12**) to the fallen of two world wars. Turn left and enter the church. At the rear, in the right hand corner, are four wall mounted plaques, dedicated to Belgian Great War servicemen. There is also a stained glass window of thanksgiving.

Return to your vehicle and go back to the bunker, turning left into Brugstraat, for the N369 junction. By the junc-

The village war memorial, commemorating two world wars.

tion with the N369, on the left, is a car park alongside a small bar; refreshments and other matters are best attended to now. From here, if you wish, walk across the busy N369, and walk a few hundred yards in the Ypres direction; on your left is the old railway bridge (**13**).

Return to your vehicle, drive over the N369 and over the canal bridge, passing a large mill on your left. You are now in the German front line, which they held from April 1915 to just before the battle of Third Ypres.

Site of the original railway bridge.

The canal side and road bridge have altered greatly since this post war photograph was taken.

Only the canal separated the opposing forces.

Follow the road round to the right, go past the first junction, ahead on the left is a large building, turn right here (facing towards Ypres). Blue signs indicate Langemark, another Ieper. You are now in Oostkaai road; when safe to do so, stop. **(14)** On your right, close to the road, is a narrow path. This was the railway embankment, now a cycle track, that served slightly further up the ridge as a boundary between the 38th (Welsh) Division and Guards Division in the attack on 31 July 1917. The immediate impression is that the embankment is much narrower and lower than expected. The track passes beyond the trees alongside the building at the junction and heads towards Langemark. Depending where you halted it is possible to see, where the track bends, that the embankment is approximately six feet above the field. On the opposite side of the road, by the builder's yard, the track leads to the canal railway bridge. If you have not already done so, walk along this short track.

Return to your vehicle, drive along Oostkaai, and where the road bends, the distant right hand ground alongside the canal is where the British line started. The road runs parallel with the canal and follows the British front line to approximately where the canal bend is. About here, the British front line turned eastwards. On the right is Boesinghe lock (**15**) *(Sluis Boezinge Dorp)*; drive in the direction of the wind turbines, passing industrial units on your right. Almost a mile along the road, just before one of the wind turbines, you will see a small sign marked Westcompost,

by a junction, with possibly flags flying from eight flagpoles. Turn left into *Bargiestraat*, you are now approximately where Barnsley Road (**16**) communication trench was. Go straight down the road and follow the bend to the left. On your right hand side is a large, dark, ultra modern building and, further along, are storage tanks; continue for roughly 200 yards. On your left hand side is a large warehouse and just before this is the site of Yorkshire Trench (**17**), situated 165 yards north of the now gone International Trench.

In 1997, during the development of the industrial site, the previously mentioned 'Diggers' discovered, between two feet and three feet below the surface, a trench system with an entrance to an underground bunker. According to a West Flanders

The 1917 trench is in the background, the wooden constructions are A frames and the duckboards in the foreground mark the route of the 1915 trench system.

The Boesinghe defenders would have liked trenches as dry and sturdy as these concreted reconstructions.

tourism book, the remains of 205 soldiers of three different nationalities were also unearthed here and re-buried in appropriate cemeteries. Ypres later acquired the open access site for the creation of a memorial in conjunction with In Flanders Fields Museum. Artefacts from the site are on display in the museum.

Yorkshire Trench was originally dug by the British in 1915 and appeared on maps from September 1916. This shallow trench seldom offered sufficient protection and possibly for this reason a new trench was created behind the existing one. Timber A frames were installed in the new trench, allowing the troops to stand above the water lined trench bottoms.

To the rear of the site is a concrete sandbag replica, tracing the 1917 route of Yorkshire Trench, complete with a sniper's loop hole and a gated entrance and exit leading to a flooded dugout. Set into the ground near the left hand entrance to the trench are eight-inch diameter steel pipes known as Livens projectors. These could fire shells containing gas, oil or explosives up to 1300 yards and now occupy the location where they were found during the excavations. Forward of the narrow replica trench, a duckboard path traces the route of the 1915 British trench and a dolomite gravel path marks the subterranean route of the dugout. Twenty minutes is sufficient time spent here.

Return to your vehicle, and proceed almost two miles, to the junction with Langemarkseweg. Facing you are three signs, turn right for Langemark, passing a Peugeot dealership on your right.

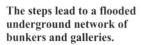

The steps lead to a flooded underground network of bunkers and galleries.

186

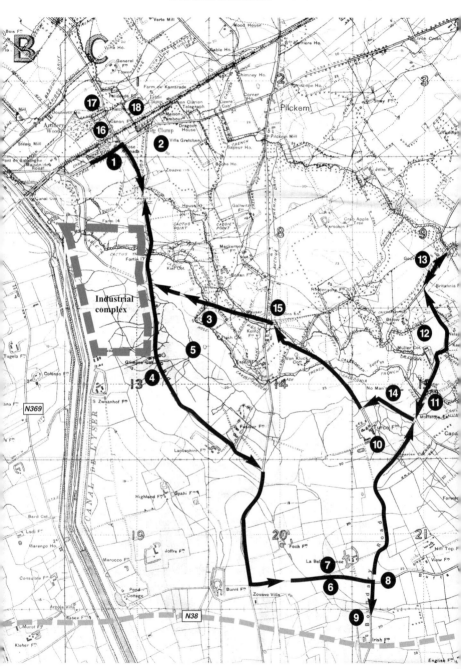

TOUR THREE

The east bank or 'sit and be hit' tour
Tour circuit distance is approximately eight miles

Away to your left you will see a row of trees and the railway embankment, this is the 38th (Welsh) Division attack zone. Continue along Langemarkseweg, you will soon see on your right a junction with a large green CWGC sign post for four cemeteries; Artillery Wood, Dragoon Camp, Welsh Cemetery (Caesar's Nose) and Colne Valley Cemetery. This is the Carrefour de la Rose or Crossroads of the Roses (**1**), pull in to the right just before the junction. **Start here.**

Memorial to gassed Algerian and French troops, shown on a 1920s postcard.

Opposite is a collection of memorials to the 45th (Algerian) Division and the French 87th (Territorial) Divisions. The latter formation consisted of ageing Breton reservists, posted to this quiet sector – until the 22 April 1915 gas attack; their positions are shown on the orientation table.

188

The crossroads of the Rose today, looking from Huddlestone Road.

After the war, the area surrounding the Crossroads of the Roses became the focus of an annual pilgrimage for Breton families whilst many of the fallen were exhumed and re-interred in their own villages. In recognition of the fallen, a small park resembling the Brittany countryside was created by the erection of a sixteenth century pink granite Brittany calvary. In front of this stands a pre-historic megalithic dolmen table, which would not look out of place at Stonehenge. Eight Brittany boulders, some bearing the names of regiments that fought here, encircle this memorial garden that was officially dedicated in September 1929. A back drop of pine trees (which now obstruct the orientation view) and a carpet of heather and broom replicated the Brittany flora.

Return to your vehicle, immediately turn right and follow the CWGC sign for Welsh Cemetery, Colne Valley and Dragoon Camp cemetery. This is Kleine Poelstraat, known to the British as Huddlestone Road; some 700 yards from this junction you will cross the German front line. The industrial park is on your right; as you see the first unit look away to your left, and in the distance there is a British cemetery. Stop as convenient.

On the left a CWGC sign directs you to Dragoon Camp Cemetery (**2**), up a very long grass track that retains water in wet weather. A track from near Dragoon House and past Villa Gretchen led to the cemetery, originally adopting the latter name. Perhaps due to the Germanic sounding name, the cemetery was renamed the more acceptable Dragoon Camp.

Part of the very long grass path leading to the isolated Dragoon Camp Cemetery.

Until the advance of the 38th (Welsh) Division on 31 July 1917, this location was behind enemy lines. On 9 August members of 13/Royal Welsh Fusiliers selected the site for the burial of their fallen comrades who were killed on the first day of the offensive; fourteen of the identified graves are from this battalion. Of the fifty-six identified graves in this cemetery, thirty-six belong to units from the Royal Welsh Fusiliers; there are also ten unidentified graves. The longest plot contains forty-six Royal Welsh Fusiliers, giving this isolated burial place a distinctly Welsh connection. The far right hand grave (B1) belongs to Major Evan Davies, fatally wounded during a 15/RWF reconnaissance raid. The 27 July 1917 raid claimed forty lives; half of these are on the Menin Gate, while others rest here in graves B1, B11, B14, B20, B21, B24 and B40. The interments continued here until October 1917.

Return to Huddlestone Road and continue south along the winding lane, past a large mobile phone mast. You will soon see a CWGC sign post, at this point you are approximately 250 yards behind British lines. Turn left into Moortelweg; the junction is slightly in front of the British line section E31. The British line was about 200 yards forward of Huddlestone Road and only seventy five yards of No Man's Land here separated the armies. A CWGC sign will direct you along a track to the German trench salient Caesar's Nose, now the site of Welsh Cemetery (Caesar's Nose) (**3**). The rough narrow track ends on private property,

Royal Welsh Fusiliers Private T H Davies, killed 27 July and Private J E Cleary, killed 31 July 1917.

and so it is best to park at the junction and walk to the cemetery.

The soldiers of the 38th (Welsh) Division began this cemetery in July 1917, after capturing the pronounced salient in the enemy line known as Caesar's Nose. Twenty-three graves belong to the division, including three Fusiliers killed in the disastrous 27 July 1917 raid. The cemetery was used until the following November; there are sixty-eight Great War graves, of which nine are unidentified. Looking towards the British line, the beginning of section E29 is on your right hand, to the left is E28 and E27 began more or less facing Colne Valley cemetery. This sector is where the Germans released chlorine gas on 19 December 1915.

Caesar's Nose Cemetery approached from the British lines.

Return to Huddlestone Road, then turn left; by a bend in the road, after a row of weeping willow type trees, is Colne Valley Cemetery (**4**), named after Colne Valley trench (C.13.a.b), which once wound its way past Glimpse Cottage (positioned on the right where the row of trees are). Today, this once isolated comrades cemetery is almost engulfed by the industrial site, and may eventually be relocated.

Late July casualties from the RWFs and Welch Regiment.

> *Colne Valley was no place to stay in, with its broken dugouts and its problem never solved, namely how to get the water which gathered there to run out of the trench and its dugouts, and not always into the same.* Major W P Wheldon DSO.

The West Riding Territorials began the cemetery in June or July 1915 and it continued to be used until the following February. There are forty-three identified graves and four unknown.

Colne Valley Cemetery, taken from Huddlestone Road.

The plot contains thirty graves of men from the Duke of Wellington's (West Riding) Regiment. On 14 August 1915, a shell landed in a dug out killing three men and wounding two other 1/4 Battalion members. Captain Maynard Percy Andrews and two stretcher-bearers, despite heavy fire, risked crossing open land to take Private Lee for urgent medical treatment. Captain Andrews died due to a bullet in the neck, the mortally wounded Private Lee also died. A French epitaph on Captain Andrew's headstone translates No man can have greater love than to give his life for a friend. Curiously, his headstone states he died a day later than the incident. The graves of this sad affair are located at C7, C9, C11 and C12. Grave C13 contains Private Aked of the 5th Battalion, who may have been in the destroyed dugout. Graves D8, 9 and 10 contain Horner, Bailey and Wade, all of the 6th Battalion, who were all fatally sniped in the head within a few hours of each other.

While standing with your back to the cemetery, look towards Welsh (Caesar's Nose) Cemetery; to the right of this is a fenced field between the near left

Headstone of Captain M P Andrews who was killed while aiding a wounded soldier.

The author and an excavated section of light railway track near Colne Valley.

Corrugated iron revetment in a flooded trench. How ironic!

hand corner of the field and Huddlestone Road. Archaeologists excavated here during the spring of 2009. Some two feet below the surface their first trench produced a section of light railway track (**5**).

The Ypres League 'Map of the Salient', shows that Glimpse Cottage railway ended at the far edge of Huddlestone Road, therefore the discovery appears to be an extension. Within the excavation, approximately twenty-five yards north of the light railway track, the archaeologists came across a Great War trench section. In keeping with our perception of Boesinghe trenches, this was also flooded, providing a twenty-first century reminder of the conditions endured by the defenders of Boesinghe. Above the water's surface, lying on its longest length, protruded a length of corrugated iron revetment. It would appear, in an attempt to discover the extent of the light railway track, archaeologists, to no apparent avail, created a trench twenty yards closer to the German line.

Now continue along Huddlestone Road in the direction of an electricity pylon. About four hundreds yards away on your right stood Lancashire Farm. The tunnelling companies sank a fifty-foot deep shaft here, with a gallery extending beneath this road to the forward positions. A partially concealed light railway transported the spoil away from the workings. The tunnel, with its integral dugouts and dressing station, removed the dangers of surface relief or forward movement across particularly hazardous terrain. An interesting paragraph in *Tunnellers* reveals how the Germans were deceived at Lancashire Farm.

When the Fifth Army attack opened on 31 July 1917 the Germans were waiting for it, but in one sector they were taken by surprise. The heap of spoil from the Lancashire Farm series of dugouts had grown to an enormous size. The Germans drew the only apparent inference – mining. Knowing our conservative methods, the Germans were convinced that, as at Messines, our attack would be preceeded by mines, the firing of which would be the signal for their [British] *artillery to open fire. But there were no mines; consequently the* [German] *barrage was late in forming, which was a decided advantage to the attacking troops – who swarmed over and captured the enemy's position all along the front...*

Continue down the road; in the far distance on the right hand side is a large blue direction sign. At the end of Huddlestone Road, turn right onto the busy Pilkemseweg (Pilkem to Ieper road), you are now heading for Ypres. After approximately half a mile, you will see on your left CWGC signs for La Belle Alliance and Divisional Collecting Post cemeteries; turn left up a narrow track. You are now in Hogeziekenweg and, from the ridge, you will see two cemeteries. On your right is La Belle Alliance Cemetery (**6**), with the larger Divisional Collecting Post Extension almost opposite. Stop beside the second cemetery.

Cross the lane and go to the small battlefield cemetery that takes its name from La Belle Alliance farmhouse, which once stood here near the

La Belle Alliance Cemetery this area was a notorious and much hated hot spot.

west end of Buffs Road. Coney Street communication trench and the light railway track to Hill Top farm ran to the right of the lane. The cemetery is sited near the south-west corner of the now gone farm, and is approximately half a mile behind the British front line of 1917. Access to this site is by a thirty-yard grass path. The burial parties of 10 and 11 Kings Royal Rifle Corps started this cemetery. The burials took place between 12 February and 2 March 1916 and recommenced from July to August 1917. There are sixty casualties, ten of them unidentified.

Here twenty-two men share double graves, whilst one headstone marks the shared grave of several unidentified South Staffordshires. The 27 July Staffordshire casualties are from the VC action involving Private Barratt (see Essex Farm tour). Two days previously seven members of this battalion died during a raid on the junction of Cake and Calabash Trench on the Pilckem Road (C.14.a). No enemy were encountered, but shellfire killed six men and wounded seven; at least one man died of wounds and they are buried here.

Now cross over to the other cemetery. The photograph of the 'iron harvest' was taken against the front wall of Divisional Collecting Post Cemetery and Extension; the munitions await collection by the bomb disposal teams.

Anonymous in death, a shared South Staffordshire grave.

Wartime relics such as shells and grenades are highly dangerous, so do not touch such objects, for it can lead to death or injury.

Divisional Collecting Post Cemetery, Boesinghe (**7**) was begun by field ambulances of the 48th (South Midland) and 58th (London)

The 'iron harvest' waiting for collection by the bomb disposal team.

Shells

Divisional Collecting Post Cemetery, the distant wind vanes are in the Boesinghe industrial park.

Divisions in August 1917 and remained in use until January 1918. By the Armistice there were eighty-six graves. However, between 1924 and 1926 the original cemetery was considerably enlarged when graves were brought in from the surrounding battlefields and small burial grounds. The cemetery and extension essentially form a single site, but the records of the original burials and concentrations were kept separately until they were combined in 2001. The original cemetery comprises Rows B to E of Plot 1 and, in addition to the original burials, special memorials have been erected to two casualties known to have been buried in Westroosebeke Churchyard, whose graves could not be located after the war. A total of eighty-eight Commonwealth Great War casualties are now buried or commemorated in the cemetery. There is one German grave. The extension consists of rows F to S of Plot One, and all of Plot Two, a total of 676 Commonwealth burials, these break down into 493 United Kingdom, 102 Australian, seventy-three Canadian, five New Zealand, two Newfoundland and one South African; of these 511 are unidentified.

New Irish Farm Cemetery is a five minutes walk away, or go by car. Continue straight ahead, you will see the Cross of Sacrifice on your right hand side as you approach the crossroads. The right hand opposite corner of this junction was known as Hammonds Corner (**8**); turn right into Briekestraatweg, once Boundary Road, and stop at the cemetery entrance. At the end of the road is the Noorderring, better known as the N38.

New Irish Farm Cemetery is notable for the number of Boesinghe

New Irish Farm Cemetery viewed from Boundary Road.

sector casualties re-interred here. Originally there was a farm near here, known to the soldiers as Irish Farm. To the south (28.C.27 a.2.5) lay Irish Farm Cemetery. The CWGC are unable to locate any details about Irish Farm Cemetery and it is assumed that the graves were transferred to New Irish Farm Cemetery (**9**), sited approximately 300 yards north of the farm. This burial plot was used from August to November 1917 and again during the crisis months of April and May 1918. The initial graves are found in the three irregular plots with Plot 1, located by the War Stone. When the guns finally ceased there were seventy-three graves. After the Armistice, 4,715 fallen Great War servicemen were brought to this 'concentration' cemetery, of which 3,276 graves are unidentified. Special Memorials record four casualties possibly buried amongst them, whilst other memorials commemorate thirty fatalities originally interred in four of the cemeteries relocated here but whose graves were lost due to shellfire.

In addition, thirty cemeteries, each containing an average of twenty graves, were relocated here, including seven burial grounds from the Boesinghe area. The CWGC enquiries department very kindly examined their records for details relating to the Boesinghe graves concentrated into this cemetery. Individual records for the concentrated cemeteries no longer exist, but some information was found after discovering the original trench map references in an old cemetery book. Using these references, they were able to find the following grave details among the 590 pages of burial details the Commission hold for this cemetery.

Admiral's Cemetery (28.C.15. c.8.7) was formerly located at the intersection of Boundary and Admiral's Road, close to No Man's Cottage. The cemetery name refers to Lieutenant Smith RN DSO, attached to the HQ of the 6th Division. The cemetery contained the graves of nineteen soldiers who died in the last two years of the conflict. The men were reburied here in Plot 16 Row F, graves 1 to 5 and Plot 18 Row E graves 1 to 20.

Fusilier Farm Cemetery (28.C.14.c.4.9), to the west of the Ypres to Pilkem road, was a comrades' cemetery commemorating seventeen men from the 38th (Welsh) Division killed on the opening day of Third Ypres. The transferred graves are in Plot 25 Row D graves 1 to 19. The epitaph on the grave (D11) of Driver James Edward Lusted, of 38th Division Ammunition Column, reads 'Sleep sweet upon the blood stained sod, dear son who has gone to God'.

Fusilier Farm Road Cemetery (28.C.13.b.9.1) contained fourteen men from the 38th (Welsh) Division who fell between 31 July and 2 August 1917. This was sited only 100 yards north-west of Fusilier Farm Cemetery. No further records were found.

Glimpse Cottage Cemetery (28.C.13.b.5.4) held eighteen graves of

The site of Turco Farm, situated off Boundary Road.

men from the 38th (Welsh) Division killed in July and August 1917. This was some 250 metres north-west of Fusilier Farm Road Cemetery. Some of the graves are in Plot 25 Row F graves 1 to 13.

Mirfield Cemetery (28.C.14.c.00.35) stood approximately 300 yards west of Fusilier Farm. Named after Mirfield Trench (C13.d.14.c), the cemetery contained the graves of sixteen United Kingdom men and, with the exception of one grave, they all belong to the 51st (Highland) Division. The dates on the wooden crosses ranged from June to August 1917. The graves are now in Plot 25 Row B graves 1 to 17.

Paratonniers Farm Cemetery (20.T.28.d.2.8), a Belgian cemetery some 800 yards south of Lizerne, contained thirteen United Kingdom casualties of the December 1917 to March 1918 period. The graves are now in Plot 31 Row A graves 4 to 10 and Plot 31 Row C graves 1 to 9.

The grave of Lieutenant Charles Lindsay Claude Bowes-Lyon, formerly interred in Boesinghe churchyard is in Plot 30 Row D Grave 2 (See Tour Two).

Pilckem Road Cemetery (28.C.14.c.8.8) was located approximately 300 yards north-west of Fusilier Farm, twenty-seven United Kingdom soldiers were first laid to rest here; of these, eighteen men belonged to 1/5 Gordon Highlanders. They were reburied in Plot 26 Row A graves 1 to 20 and Plot 26 Row B graves 1 to 7.

Return to your vehicle, turn around, go back along Boundary Road and at the junction go straight ahead. At this point, on the left edge of the road, ran Gawthorpe Road Trench, which ran in a straight line, whereas the road bows outwards before returning to run parallel with this trench. In less than half a mile you will approach, on your left, a sharp right-hand bend. Facing you, but set back from the road, is a long building accessed by a tree lined lane. Opposite is a small but convenient place to stop.

You are roughly two hundred yards behind the British front line. The large building positioned centrally across the access lane stands approximately on the site of Turco Farm (**10**). Trench maps show that the original farm buildings were to the right of the lane, the trench railway from Austerlitz Farm terminated to the left of it. When you stand on the bend, looking towards the farm, at a point midway along the lane and approximately two hundreds to the left was Knaresborough Castle. Between there and the farm ran Pump Room trench, where the gallantry of Corporal Samuel Meekosha was recognised by the award of the Victoria Cross. Major W P Wheldon DSO wrote:

> *Turco was another stronghold sure but, to the ignorant observer, it might have contained a shrine of some great holiness, so precipitately and incessantly did all those who approached it prostrate themselves into the mud around. But these devotees did reverence only to a German machine gun.*

Return to your vehicle and follow the road up the ridge. On your left stands a red brick house situated at Moortelweg crossroad. Midway between the junction and the last halt, the D18 section of the British line was to the right of the road, before angling acutely forward towards a point some forty yards shy of the intersecting junction. The line then crossed the road; this was the start of the D19 section. The junction was known as Morteledje Estaminet, and the road dipping away to your right is Admiral's Road. At the corner of the house are two CWGC

The junction known as Morteledje Estaminet today.

The British line facing Morteledje Estaminet.

BRITISH FRONT LINE

BOUNDARY ROAD

The German front line Calendar Trench crossed the road where the track is.

signs. The left sign is for No Man's Cot Cemetery, the other is for Minty Farm Cemetery. Go straight ahead, until you see a small cattle shelter on the right of the road, pull in on your right. The track running in front of the shelter corresponds with a section of German front line known as Calender Trench (**11**) (C.15 central).

Carry on in the direction you were travelling; in a bend on the road you pass a farm built near the site of Muller Cot. The road bends sharply to the right, pull in at the next junction, and walk back a bit. Between this farm and Below Farm in the rear of their front line, and 250 yards from the front lines, the Germans constructed the infamous redoubt High Command (**12**). Due to the farm and fields with cattle, it is not possible to look back to the Boesinghe lines, but notice Admiral's Road leading towards the N38. The green bank at the end of the A19 is almost a mile distant and to the right, behind the pylon, is Track X Cemetery, which was between the lines in June 1917. With a height above sea level of over twenty-seven metres, some seven metres higher than Caesar's Nose, and over seventeen metres above the canal, from this point German gunners witnessed all before them. As you return to your vehicle, notice the sections of light railway and barbed wire stanchions surrounding a field.

Continue along Boundary Road until you reach a junction signposted Langemark. Ignore the CWGC sign for Minty Farm, turn left into Briekestraat, for Langemark. To the left of the road is where the 1/KSLI counter attacked on 21/22 April 1916. As you go down the slope, look away to your right. In between a cluster of buildings, you will see in the distance a large, greyish white, dairy processing plant. The extreme left of this building is by the Steenbeek, the limit of the Guards Division's advance on 31 July 1917. The road bends into Vanheulestraat; after a few hundred yards, on the left, you pass farm buildings, fronted by pollarded trees. Immediately after the farm stands the formidable Goumier Farm Bunker (**13**), also named Gournier Farm on trench maps.

A still defiant looking Goumier Farm bunker.

This was simply a farmhouse, until the Germans enclosed the brick walls in thick concrete. After the 38th (Welsh) Division seized Pilckem Ridge, Royal Engineers modified and reinforced the walls; thick concrete blast walls were also constructed. During the spring offensive of 1918 the Germans captured the bunker for a while until the Black Watch finally ousted them. Above one of the doorways is a plaque: 'In memory of comrades of 38th (Welch) Division 1914-18'.

Turn around and head back towards Morteledje Crossroads; just before the junction you pass through Duck's Bill. Turn right into Moortelweg, on the corner of a house is a CWGC sign for No Man's Cot Cemetery. The British line was near your left, and you are driving through an area that was for much of the war No Man's Land. In less than half a mile a CWGC sign on the left points across the field to No Man's Cot

A cyclist, at more or less the forward limit of the Duck's Bill, all unknowing heads towards the German lines.

No Man's Cot Cemetery, looking to the British lines that ran close to the opposite side of the road.

Cemetery (**14**), accessed by a 175 yards long grass track. For much of the war the site of the cemetery and surrounding fields was No Man's Land. It owes its name to a building situated on the south side of Admiral's Road and was used as a cemetery from July 1917 to March 1918. There are seventy seven identified United Kingdom graves and two unknowns here. Over fifty percent of the graves belong to officers and men from the 51st (Highland) Division.

Return to your car and proceed for nearly half a mile; take care, on your right is an ivy-clad building sited on the corner of a major road junction. This is the crossroads known as Five Chemins Estaminet (**15**), and was roughly 400 yards behind enemy lines until the summer of 1917. Go across the junction into Moortelweg and, about 500 yards on the left, you will pass the gravel track leading to Welsh (Caesar's Nose) Cemetery. Continue down the slope; the way ahead will be familiar. At the junction turn right into Huddlestone Road, and meet the Carrefour de la Rose junction, just over two miles from Morteledje Crossroads.

Go straight ahead, and park clear of the junction. Slightly ahead and on your left is the former railway embankment, now a cycle path, which meets the road here. A few yards to your left, bushes surround the memorial to the poet Lance Corporal Francis Ledwidge (**16**), who was killed on this spot on 31 July 1917. The yellow brick memorial was unveiled on 31 July 1998. There are two transparent panels, one bears an image of Ledwidge above the first two lines of *The Lament for Thomas McDonagh*, a friend and fellow poet, executed after the Dublin 1916 Easter Rebellion. The other panel displays his 1917 poem, *Soliloquy*.

Walk or drive about 100 yards along Poezelstraat to Artillery Wood Cemetery (**17**). This is roughly half a mile east of the Yser canal and just north of Artillery Wood, which was never replanted. The Guards Division created this cemetery for the interment of their comrades killed during the

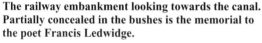

The railway embankment looking towards the canal. Partially concealed in the bushes is the memorial to the poet Francis Ledwidge.

attack up Pilckem Ridge. Every infantry unit of the Guards Division is represented here and it was later used as a front line cemetery for all units until March 1918. By November of that year the cemetery contained 141 graves, including forty-two Royal Artillery men, killed whilst operating the nearby batteries. After the Armistice the cemetery was expanded considerably, when graves were relocated here, including nineteen soldiers, mainly guardsmen, killed during the June to August 1917 fighting, originally buried in Boesinghe Chateau cemetery. A further twenty-two United Kingdom soldiers, originally buried in a French military cemetery north of Langemarck, were moved here. A further sixty-three United Kingdom graves, located at Captain's Farm Cemetery, west of Langemarck, were also transferred here. The dead were primarily from the 29th and Guards Divisions killed between July 1917 and the following March. Isolated battlefield graves and other small burial plots around Boesinghe were also concentrated to this site, taking the total to 1,307 Great War casualties commemorated or buried within this cemetery; of these only 801 are identified.

In Plot 3. Row D Grave 12 lies the first 1/4 Duke of Wellington's officer killed. Lieutenant E Lee was shot through the head while instructing some of his men of the Machine Gun Section to repair a weak spot in the parapet.

Arguably the two most illustrious Celtic poets of their generation are

203

also here. Francis Edward Ledwidge was born 19 August 1887, in Slane, County Meath, Ireland. He worked as a labourer and became active in trade unionism. Ledwidge was a keen poet and in 1910 the *Drogheda Independent* published the first of his work. Other commissions followed and aided by the patronage of the local aristocrat Lord Dunsay, the 'navvy poet's' career blossomed.

Francis Ledwidge.

Ledwidge was a keen supporter of full Irish independence but, unexpectedly, on 24 October 1914, the poet enlisted into the Royal Inniskilling Fusiliers. He served with the 5th Battalion in the Gallipoli and Salonika campaigns, until he suffered a back problem. After a period of recuperation in hospital, Ledwidge returned to Ireland. In December 1916 he went to France with a draft of 1/Royal Inniskilling Fusiliers. The following summer his battalion arrived in the Salient. On 31 July, Ledwidge and others from B Company worked through pouring rain, repairing the Boesinghe to Pilckem road in readiness for the artillery advance. Ledwidge and five others had stopped work for a warming cup of tea when a random shell exploded in their midst. The Celtic poet was originally buried at Carrefour de Rose, and now lies here in grave Plot 2 Row B Grave 5.

Nearby, in Plot 2 Row F Grave 11, rests Ellis Humphrey Evans, who was born in January 1887, the eldest of eleven sons, to hill farmer parents. On leaving school he tended sheep on the family farm at Penlan, Transfynydd, Merioneth. Young Ellis 'wrote prose as easily as breathing'. While reciting at a local Eisteddfod competition, his face was bathed in a shaft of sunlight; this, and his impact on his elders, resulted in the bestowal of the bardic name of Hedd Wynn (Perfect Peace).

Most farmers were exempt from military service but, as the war progressed, the Evans farm was considered to be over manned. In February 1917, when one of the younger brothers received his call up papers, Hedd Wynn volunteered to take his place. He served as 61117 Private Evans with 15/Royal Welsh Fusiliers and, while undergoing training, completed his entry for the 1917 Birkenhead Eisteddfod. His poem, *Yr Arwr* (The Hero), was submitted under the *non-de plume* of

Fleur de Lys. The week long Eisteddfod began on 5 September 1917, culminating in the announcement of *Fleur de Lys* as the champion of free verse. No winner stepped forward, for Private Ellis Humphrey Evans was killed on 31 July 1917 on Pilkem Ridge. The traditional Eisteddfod prize, an elaborately carved chair, was draped with black cloth in memory of the fallen soldier and became symbolic of the empty seats in family homes throughout the country.

Against the headstone of Second Lieutenant David Charles Phillips, who was attached to 2/RWF when he was killed on 16 August 1917, is a poignant private memorial. The parents of the twenty-two year old appear to have run the Albion Arms in Llanelly. In June 1928 or 29 (some of the last digit is missing due to damage) the bereaved family visited his grave in Plot 5 Row A and left the plaque. In Plot 7 Row A Grave 14 lies a RFA gunner who served with 5/56 Trench Mortar Battery. The headstone of Private Thomas Frederick Riches records 'Killed in action at Boesinghe 18 July 1917'.

The grave of Second Lieutenant D C Phillips with a plaque placed in the late 1920s by his bereaved family.

Whilst standing in Poezelstraat with your back to the cemetery, look through gaps in the houses or use the cycle track. Away to the right and bounded by the higher and parallel Slaakestrant is where Sergeant Robert James Bye VC 1/Welsh Guards tackled block houses. Return to your vehicle and go back to the main road. For the next tour turn left and head up Pilckem Ridge.

Artillery Wood Cemetery in the 1920s.

TOUR FOUR

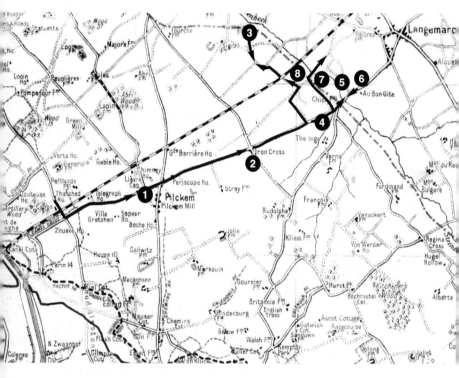

The 31 July 1917 advance towards Langemark
Tour circuit is approximately four miles

Start here. Drive up Boezingestraat, following the signs for Langemark. After a half a mile, you cross the barely noticeable Corner House crossroads (**1**), the site of a VC action. Carry on, after 150 yards is Pilckem Crossroads, intersected by Pilkemseweg and distinguishable by a bar on the left. After half a mile you reach Iron Cross crossroads. On the left is De Sportman Bar, diagonally opposite this is a modern bus stop. On the nearby wall hangs a Welsh flag above a small blue slate plaque, commemorating Hedd Wynn (**2**), who was fatally wounded here on 31 July 1917. The memorial was unveiled on the seventy-fifth anniversary of his death.

Continue in the same direction and roughly 600 yards later, turn left at the CWGC sign for Ruisseau Farm Cemetery (**3**); you are now just over three miles from Boesinghe station. Go straight down the lane and about

700 yards on the right is the CWGG cemetery sign, turn into Melkerijftraat and head for the farmhouse. The cemetery is accessed through the farm, so please park sensibly in the farm back yard. There is a large dog here, usually confined to a wire compound.

With your back to the farmhouse, just beyond the cemetery, the 2/Coldstream Guard frontage arched away to align with the Third Objective, an imaginary line 100 yards forward of the Iron Cross to Kortekeer Cabaret road. After the 20 September capture of Langemark, the 1/Irish Guards assembled here for their 9 October 1917 attack across the Broembeek. The cemetery was begun after this 'small but successful operation'. Later burials were made by artillery units and the cemetery continued to be used until November 1917. There are eighty-two Great War dead here, including six unidentified men.

Return the half mile back to the main road, turn left, and follow Boezingestraat up the ridge. After several hundred yards you will reach Cement House Cemetery (**4**), Langemarck, named after a fortified building sited on this road. (The huge Cement House is in the confines of the adjacent farm, concealed by greenery.)

The 4th and 17th Divisional burial officers began the cemetery in August 1917. Field Ambulances and other units buried their dead here until April 1918.

The memorial to Hedd Wyn at the location of his death in 1917.

After the Armistice, the dead from over a dozen cemeteries were concentrated here. Plots sixteen, seventeen and eighteen originally contained about 500 French graves, but these were removed in 1922. The

Ruisseau Farm Cemetery, viewed looking towards the Steenbeek.

vacated space has been used over the intervening years for graves brought in from communal cemeteries. The cemetery is open for the burial of remains that continue to be discovered. The expansion is evident in Plot 1 Row H, where the original end of row headstone of Private H McAdam bears on its side IH. Over the years a further twenty-one graves have been added to the row and extend to the right of McAdam. In November 2005 the remains of nine unidentified British soldiers, discovered by the 'Diggers' at the Boesinghe excavation, were interred here. The graves are in Plot 1 Row H.

At the time of writing, there are 3,583 Commonwealth Great War servicemen buried or commemorated in this cemetery, of whom 2,416 are unidentified. There are also twenty-two Second World War graves here. Assuming the cemetery visitor book gives an indication of numbers visiting the site, I was surprised to see that, since my visit twelve months earlier, only six pages of the small book separated my two visits.

Resume your journey towards Langemark; when you come to a junction with large chevrons, go straight ahead, passing Ieperstraat on your right. The road soon crosses the Steenbeek, where an Albertina Memorial (**5**) commemorates the ending of the Steenbeek offensive on 28 September 1918.

Stop here, as either side of the bridge affords good views of the 38th (Welsh) Division objective. A few hundred yards to the left was the imaginary boundary with the 51st Division. A few hundred yards along the road, on the left, stands the tall 20th (Light) Division memorial (**6**).

Cement House Cemetery, Langemarck, shown in the 1920s. This cemetery continues to receive the remains of Great War servicemen, now usually discovered during the construction of roads and property.

The Steenbeek was successfully crossed on 31 July 1917. Successive counter attacks were repulsed, but a hundred yards away at Bon-Gite, the Germans drove a party of 11 South Wales Borderers (2nd Gwent Pals) back to the left hand bank in this area.

Now return to the junction, turn right into Milkweg. Near the dairy processing plant is a right hand bend, pull in onto a wide track. Leave your car here. A few yards away, alongside the Steenbeek, are two low posts flanking a small slate memorial. Private (and Lewis gunner) Harry Patch, (7) C Company 7/Duke of Cornwalls Light Infantry, who had the distinction of being the last British veteran of the Great War trenches, unveiled this memorial here in September 2008. Part of the plaque inscription states: At dawn on 16 August 1917, the 7/DCLI crossed here for the successful attack on Langemark.

The 20th (Light) Division memorial today, now flanked by houses.
The 20th (Light) Division memorial in the 1920s

Walk towards the arched bridge and the embankment/ cycle track. The problems posed by the embankment to the British now become obvious.

The Steenbeek, the railway embankment is on the left horizon.

Walk onto the embankment (**8**); on your left extends the 1,000 yard front gained by the 38th (Welsh) Division on 31 July. Immediately to your right, 2/Grenadier Guards held the far river bank, now a factory site. Walk west along the cycle path for a full appreciation of the ground attacked; the road you see crossing the track leads to Ruisseau Farm. Return to your

A close up of the commemorative tablet.

The Harry Patch memorial to his comrades, with Langemark church spire in the distance.

Here, at dawn, on 16 August 1917, the 7th Battalion, Duke of Cornwall's Light Infantry, 20th (Light) Division, crossed the Steenbeek prior to their successful assault on the village of Langemarck.

This stone is erected to the memory of fallen comrades and to honour the courage, sacrifice and passing of the Great War generation. It is the gift of former Private, Lewis Gunner Harry Patch, No. 29295, C Company, 7th DCLI, the last surviving veteran to have served in trenches of the Western Front.

September 20

'We weren't heroes. We didn't want to be there. We were scared. We all were, all the time. And any man who tells you he wasn't is a damn liar.'
HARRY PATCH
17 JUNE 1898
25 JULY 2009

The Steenbeek and the embankment that acted as a divisional boundary.

2/Grenadier Guards progressed approximately 200 yards eastwards beyond the right hand bank.

Looking north from the embankment across part of the terrain gained by the Guards on 31 July 1917. 2/Grenadier Guards crossed the Steenbeek near here.

transport and drive approximately one and a half miles to Corner House crossroads, just past Pilckem Crossroads.

TOUR FIVE

A short tour to two gas memorials, a huge German bunker and a VC action site

Tour circuit is approximately four miles

As you proceed down the ridges you pass Pilckem Crossroads, now look on your left for a shop facing an undeveloped corner, turn right and park where safe. **Start here.** (**1**) This junction is Corner House Crossroads, where a pillbox stalled the 13/RWF advance until Corporal James Davies captured the pillbox. The Fusiliers advanced but another machine gun, concealed in Corner House itself, blocked the advance.

Corporal James L Davies

Corporal Davies led a small group, charged the post and silenced the weapon. For these and other acts of gallantry performed on 31 July, Corporal Davies received a posthumous Victoria Cross.

Corner House crossroads where the heroism of Corporal James L Davies led to his awarding of a posthumous Victoria Cross.

Return to your vehicle, carry on along the road, cross the cycle track and immediately turn left, by a hairpin bend warning sign. From here you have a good view of the German held ground facing Boesinghe; the church spire acts as a good landmark. After half a mile you pass a big farm with a conifer lined driveway; nearly half a mile further along Slaaktestraat, on your left, is a farmhouse, and next to this is the Zeigler Bunker. (**2**) Stop here, but take care, as a ditch runs very close to the right hand edge of the road.

The Ziegler Bunker.

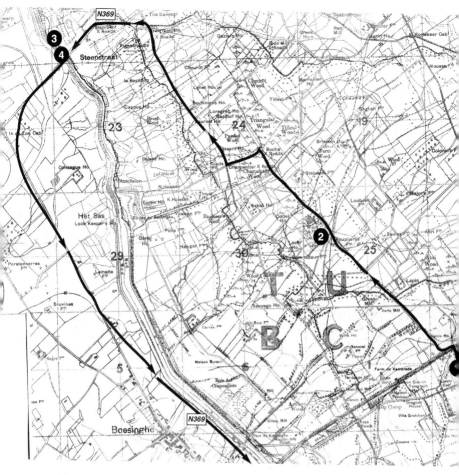

This reinforced concrete German signalling bunker stands parallel to the canal. Built during the winter of 1915-16, the structure is reputedly named after the officer who directed its construction. The French captured the bunker on 31 July 1917 and the Royal Engineers later modified the structure.

Proceed down the road and after half a mile turn left into Sastraat, now heading towards Boesinghe. At the traffic island, turn right and go past a bungalow with two white horse statues outside. At a minor crossroads there is a sign 'Poeselstraat', turn left and head for the main road. At the junction turn left, at this point you are about two and a half miles from the Ziegler Bunker. The N369 leads into Steenstratte; follow the road up the incline and, after crossing the canal, prepare to turn right into Grenadierstraat, which is on the near corner of the Cross of

213

Two of the larger and more prominent war memorials in the locality.

The Cross of Reconciliation.

The Belgian Grenadiers Memorial to the gas victims of 22 April 1915.

Reconciliation site. A few hundred yards from the junction, on the left hand side of the road, two flags fly either side of a tall obelisk, the Belgian Grenadiers Regiment Memorial.(**3**)

Now go back to the junction and turn right, immediately stopping alongside the fifteen metre high aluminium Cross of Reconciliation (**4**), dedicated to the 418th *Regiment d'Infanterie Francais*, the first victims of gas asphyxiation. This French memorial, inaugurated on 25 June 1961, is a replacement for the 1929 original, destroyed in 1942 by Third Reich troops, who took exception to its reference to German barbarians. The stonework around the grassed mound now commemorates other battalions. This visit concludes the tour.

Drive straight ahead and follow the N369 signs for Ypres; this route will take you past Boesinghe and the cemeteries we visited earlier.

TOUR SIX

A selective circular tour of the Rear Areas of approximately nineteen miles

If you intend starting this tour from Ypres, take the N38 towards Poperinghe. Alternatively, if you are beginning this tour immediately after concluding Tour Five, proceed about five miles towards Ypres. Passing Essex Farm Cemetery but before the road bridge, you need to turn right to join the N38, heading in the direction of Poperinghe. The modern road sweeps in a great arc around Vlamertinghe. Once the road straightens out and runs parallel with the railway look out for Brandhoek hamlet on your right, this is about four miles from Essex Farm. The N38 bisects Brandhoek and the motorist needs to turn left at the junction for the southern half of Brandhoek, please take care as this is a fast road. This leads into Branderstraat and immediately on your left is Brandhoek Military Cemetery. During the war this area was relatively safe from artillery fire and consequently Field Ambulances were located here for most of the war. This cemetery was begun in May 1915 in a field adjoining one of the dressing stations. The cemetery remained in use until July 1917. There are 669 graves here, comprising 601 United Kingdom, sixty-two Canadian, four Australian, two Bermudian, one German, and three unknown burials. After paying your respects, go down the lane on your right.

Headstone of N G Chavasse VC and Bar MC.

About 300 yards along the lane a CWGC sign directs you to turn right along a narrow pedestrian access path to Brandhoek New Military Cemetery (**1**). Go past the sign, park alongside the cemetery on the left and walk back to the sign. The cemetery now sited behind houses began after Brandhoek Military Cemetery closed. Interments were carried out here between July and August 1917. There are 514 United Kingdom, eleven Australian, six Canadian and twenty-eight German burials. The cemetery contains one of the most visited graves on the Western Front (Plot 3 Row B Grave 15), that of Captain Noel Godfrey Chavasse VC and Bar, MC, Royal Army Medical Corps.

The Battalion Medical Officer of the Liverpool Scottish was awarded his first Victoria Cross for his deeds at Guillemont, on the Somme, in 1916. On 2 August 1917 'The Doc', while displaying great gallantry, was mortally wounded on the battlefield east of Wieltje and evacuated by light railway to 32 CCS Brandhoek, where he died on 4 August. He received a posthumous bar to his VC, one of only three men ever win a ban.

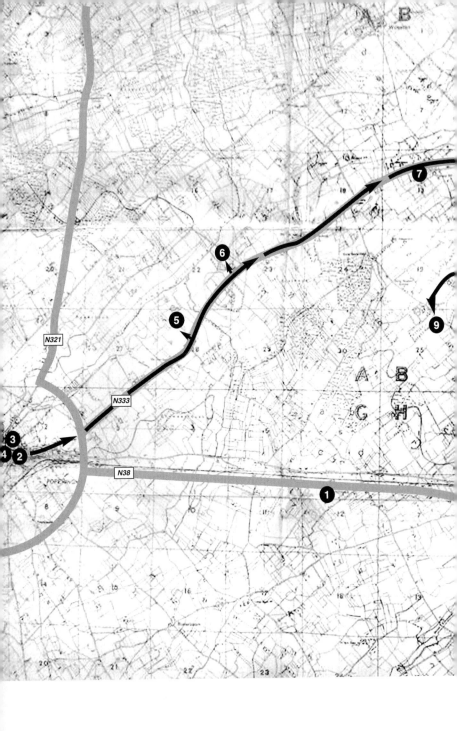

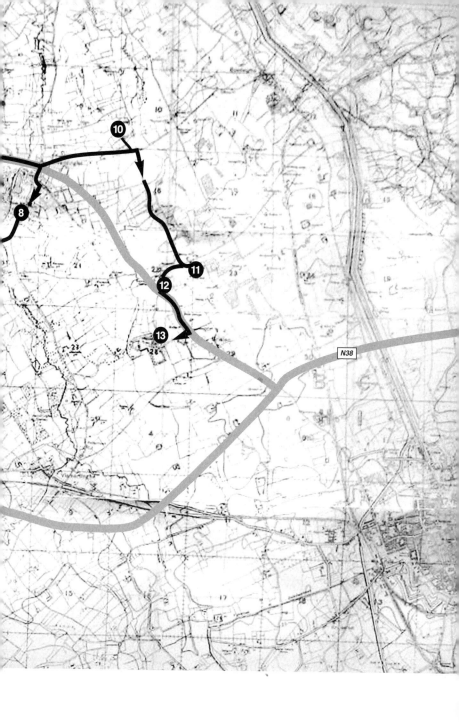

The headstone of Second Lieutenant F J Wright of the Liverpool Irish.

Next to the poppy covered grave of Captain Chavasse is another officer, Second Lieutenant Frederick John Wright of the Liverpool Irish, who received his commission on 25 January 1917, aged eighteen. Ann Clayton, the biographer of Noel Chavasse, says that this young officer was wounded on 31 July and lingered on for four days at 32 CCS. Chavasse and another officer, who may have been Second Lieutenant Wright, received Holy Communion together at 4.30 am on 4 August. It is possible Wright was the last man to ever see or speak to Chavasse. Both officers were buried on 5 August. In Plot 6 Row B Grave 11 is 356629 Private Charles Arundel Rudd, a twenty-year old 10/KLR soldier who served as batman to Chavasse. Wounded on the same day as Chavasse, the St Helens soldier succumbed to his wounds on 10 August. Return to the road and go back to your vehicle parked outside the cemetery, we now visit.

Brandhoek New Military Cemetery No 3 was begun in August when the other cemeteries were full and in the same month that the 32nd, 3rd Australian and 44th CCS arrived in the area. Burials continued until May 1918. There are 849 United Kingdom, fifty four Canadian, forty six Australian, eighteen Indian, five South African, one Britsh West Indies, four French and one Chinese burials here. All three cemeteries were designed by Sir Reginald Blomfield.

Return to the junction with the N38 and turn left, joining the traffic heading towards Poperinghe. On your right the N38 runs almost parallel with the rail track and beyond this is the old Poperinghe to Ypres road, once lined by camps, medical units and dumps. As you enter Poperinghe follow the signs for Centrum and park in the main square; beware of Saturday market day. Parking is also available outside the station. There are plenty of good restaurants, bars and even a fish and chip shop. During the Great War 'Pop' became a major hub in the British war effort and,

Poperinghe station 'the last stop before Hell'.

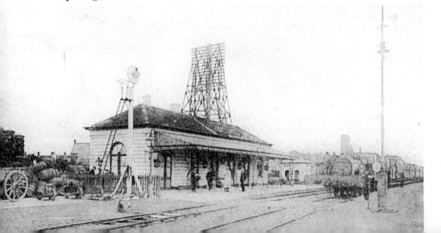

despite being sporadically shelled, the town offered a respite from the horrors of trench life. Military command headquarters, administration centres, billets and a host of military departments were housed here. The main line station was a major arrival and departure point for Salient troops, at least until 1917, and understandably it soon became known as 'the last stop before Hell'.

The following experiences of an anonymous heavy gunner featured in the *Twenty Years After* magazine.

> *I remember vividly enough my own particular fear, as my train from the base crawled into Poperinghe one evening in the spring of 1915, and I watched the Very lights going up all around the Salient. I feared then, above all, not that I should run away but that I should show to others that I wanted to run away.*
>
> *That very night I wanted to run away. Two hours after I reported for duty I was ordered to take ammunition to the guns firing from Brielen. At a spot of evil repute known as Dawson's Corner we were heavily shelled and had to gallop for it. It was my baptism of fire – the first time I had ever heard a shot fired in anger. I did not like it at all.*

The town had a pre war civilian population of 12,000 but in 1917 it was calculated 250,000 soldiers were billeted in the area. A diverse range of cafes, estaminets, theatres and hostelries provided comforts for officers or other ranks; some of these premises have survived the passage of time. The impressive, ecclesiastical looking, Town Hall overlooks the town

Despite being well behind the lines, Poperinghe was still within range of heavy artillery.

square (or Grote Markt). This was a wartime Divisional Headquarters. Today the basement contains the tourist information office, which is closed on Sunday and national holidays and for lunch between noon and one. The staff are friendly, most speak English and a range of tourist information is available.

To the left of the town hall is Gezellestraat; walk along here and, to the rear of the town hall, turn right into a courtyard. Against the right hand wall is a wooden execution post (**2**), allegedly last used in May 1919 for the execution of murderer Wang Ch'un Ch'ih, who was a Chinese labourer employed by the British army. Alongside is a polished steel plaque bearing a Rudyard Kipling epitaph:

One of the cells used by the military, usually referred to as the death cells.

I could not look on Death, which being known, Men led me to him, blindfold and alone.

As you go back to the road, under an arch you pass on your left a red door, which leads to small prison cells. The opening hours are between 9.00 am and 5.30 pm and access is free. The right hand cells look out into the courtyard, and it is likely that some men were incarcerated here awaiting execution. The military also used the cells for confining less serious offenders, who awaited transfer elsewhere for military justice to be dispensed.

Return to the main square, bear right, following the one way system towards Gasthuisstraat, passing the new La Poupee Tea Room and Restaurant (**3**). On the wall below a black coach lamp is a large diamond shaped plaque stating that the facade of the La Fabrique Café is one of very few not to have been affected by the war or been changed since then. To the soldiers the Café De L'Esperance (number seventeen) was known as 'What Opes'. The house next door (number sixteen) was 'A La Poupee'. It

An execution post, reputed to date from 1919.

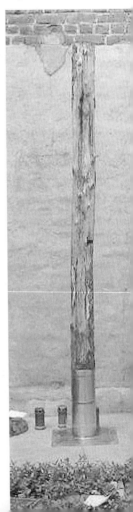

was the favourite restaurant in 'Pop' and was for officers only. The secret of La Poupee's success was Madame's hospitality and the youth of her three daughters. Ginger, the youngest, was wise beyond her thirteen to fifteen years, and was the darling of many customers. It is striking to see how often she appears in the diaries of officers who stayed in Poperinghe for a while.

Continue along Gashuisstraat, past a very useful Spar shop, and from a building a couple of hundred yards on the right hangs a sign; 'Talbot House 1915-? Every Man's Club'. Inside this eighteenth century hop merchant's house, army chaplains Philip (Tubby) Clayton and Neville Talbot established an 'Every Man's Club', open to all regardless of rank. Officially opened in December 1915 and named after Neville's brother, Lieutenant Gilbert Talbot, who was killed at Hooge in July 1915, Talbot House or Toc H (**4**), as it became known, went on to become the most popular and famous soldiers' club of the war. Whether a man required a cup of tea, a visit to the chapel, cinema, concert hall or a stroll in a quintessential English style garden, Talbot House fulfilled all these needs. In 1919 Tubby Clayton founded here the Christian Toc H charitable movement. Walk past the front door and turn right into Pottestraat where in numbers five to seven Talbot House has a museum. An entrance fee is required (currently eight Euros for adults) and the museum is closed on Mondays. Talbot House also offers basic self-catering accommodation, ideal for anyone wishing to sample the **Talbot House.** atmosphere of Toc H.

Return to Gashuisstraat and turn right, about fifty yards away on your right is a private house that once had a sign, Skindles, above the door. This is often mistaken for the original wartime establishment, once sited

beyond the mini roundabout in what is now Casselstraat. The original officer's restaurant was likened to a then famous hotel in Maidenhead, prompting the Belgian owners to re-name their premises Skindles.

During the 1920s this building opened as a hotel for battlefield tourists and adopted

In the 1920s Skindles Hotel catered for battlefield visitors.

Canada Farm Cemetery, Elverdinghe.

the well established name of the wartime officer's haunt. Turn left and walk up Priesterstraat, passing St- Bertinus' church as you return to the Grote Markt and your vehicle. Follow the one-way system through the town, on reaching the outer ring road follow the signs for the N333 and Elverdinghe.

After a mile, you pass on your left a sign for Gwalia Cemetery (**5**). Should you wish to make this optional visit, be aware that this cemetery has a 450 yard grassed access path, unsuitable for vehicles and difficult for wheelchair users. The cemetery was sited behind Gwalia Farm in an area of flat ground used for army camps by the infantry and field ambulances. The cemetery was begun in early July 1917 and continued in use until September 1918. In Plot 1 Row H are buried fourteen men of 9/Lancashire Fusiliers who were killed early on the morning of 4 September 1917 during a German air raid on Dirty Bucket Camp, near Hospital Farm. The cemetery contains 467 Commonwealth First World War burials.

On the same side of the road, approximately half a mile beyond Gwalia Farm, a CWGC sign by a farm will direct you to turn left off the N333 into Elzendammestraat, taking you behind the farm to Canada Farm Cemetery (**6**). You are now five miles north west of Ypres and less than four miles from Poperinghe station. The cemetery is a legacy of a farmhouse dressing station that existed here, from June to October 1917, for the treatment of Third Ypres casualties. There are 879 United Kingdom, five Canadian, four Newfoundlander and nineteen British West Indies troops interred here.

One of these is Edward Hornby Shears, who was educated in the Wirral and Berkshire. The eldest son of Mr and Mrs Charles Shears, of Liverpool and Birkenhead, he graduated from Trinity College, Oxford in July 1913. In August he entered the higher division of the Home Civil Service and the following year became private secretary to the Postmaster-General. In May 1915 he obtained a temporary commission in the Royal West Surrey Regiment, but a transfer to the Irish Guards followed in October 1916, and he went to the front two months later. While in the line near Boesinghe with 1/Irish Guards he received a fatal blow from a shell splinter and died on 4 July 1917 (incorrectly stated as 2 July in the Regimental history) and now lies in I A 7.

Lieutenant E H Shears and his headstone.

Six headstones commemorating eight victims of the 20 December 1915 gas attack.

Another officer casualty with a Boesinghe connection is Second Lieutenant Norman Herbert Kimpton 1st (London) Brigade Royal Field Artillery (I C 28). The Londoner was attached to Z/56 Trench Mortar

Battery. While at Boesinghe he was mortally wounded by shell fire, succumbing to his wounds on 14 July. James Llewellyn Davies VC also lies here (2 B 18). Although his headstone bears the date 31 July 1917, his family have paperwork informing them that he died of his wounds the next day.

Return to the N333 (also known as Elverdingseweg) and turn left towards Elverdinghe, the N333 soon crosses into a neighbouring commune and becomes Steenjemolenstraat. After about one and a half miles Ferme-Olivier Cemetery (**7**) is on the right hand side of the road, roughly one mile west of Elverdinghe.

Between 9 June 1915 and 5 August 1917 the 9th, 11th, 16th, 62nd, 129th and 130th Field Ambulances were successively located near by. The graves in Plot Three run in chronological order, testimony to the successive occupation of Elverdinghe Chateau by the 38th (Welsh) the Guards divisions and units of the Royal Artillery.

Corporal J L Davies VC.

Ferme-Olivier Cemetery, Elverdinghe.

The 3/Monmouth Pioneers arrayed as if they were still on parade.

In Plot Two are the graves of thirty seven men of the 3/Monmouthshires killed on 29 December 1915 by a shell whilst on parade at Elverdinghe Chateau. Due to the carnage inflicted, fourteen of the Monmouthshires share seven graves. Not far away, in Plot 2 Row B Grave 4, is Captain Purefoy Gauntlett Huddleston, 84th Field Company Royal Engineers, killed during the night of 25 March 1916. Whilst Captain Huddleston, accompanied by a 12/King's Liverpool sergeant and a private, patrolled the British wire, an alert British sentry challenged the trio. A strong wind may have drowned out the reply and, taking no chances, the sentry fired, killing the officer and 29829 Private John Wilson Carrit, who is commemorated on the Menin Gate. Also in Plot 2 Row B Grave 2 lies Captain John Chamberlain of 3/SWB, killed on 14 May 1917 whilst attached to 14/Welsh. His headstone records, 'Killed in the trenches at Boesinghe'.

There are also two executed men here. Private G Watkins 13/Welsh, was executed on 15 May 1917, following a three month period of desertion; he is buried in Plot 3 Row C Grave 12. Another deserter lies in Plot 3 Row G Grave 12; Private R Hope, 1/Inniskilling Fusiliers, faced the firing squad on 5 July 1917.

Probably most of the units once located near Boesinghe are represented within this cemetery. There are 408 Great War Commonwealth graves; of these six are unidentified and there are three German graves.

Now drive to Elverdinghe, ignoring the sharp left hand turn for the N8, and after 300 yards there is a crossroads; turn right here. Go down the road, turn left, then take the next right into Vlamertingsestraat. The grounds of Elverdinghe Chateaus (**8**) are immediately on your right; go

Elverdinghe Chateau, rebuilt after the war and visible from the road. Note the make-shift spring board and high diving platform.

226

Hospital Farm Cemetery, an isolated and peaceful final resting place.

to the gateway the chateau is visible in the distance. The lake is concealed in a dip in the grounds, whilst trees that gave the building its protection are still in abundance. This is private property, so please do not enter the grounds.

Some 600 yards further along Vlamertingsestraat is Bridge Junction; turn right here into Hospitalstraat. After approximately three-quarters of a mile you reach a junction. Turn left, and Hospital Farm Cemetery is on your right behind the nearby farm. Park in the area by the gate and follow the tree lined path for some distance across a field frequently containing livestock. Another gate leads to a small bridge across a beek and the entrance proper to the cemetery (**9**). A building here was used as a dressing station during 1915 and 1917. There are 115 United Kingdom burials, including twenty-five men from the 49th (West Riding) Division mortally wounded in 1915, and one French civilian. Hospital Farm was also used as a headquarters by various divisions, including the 49th (West Riding) Division. Their headquarters were re-located here after the 16 July 1915 wounding of Major General Baldock outside Brielen Chateau.

There are no plots in this isolated cemetery, just rows. In Row A Grave 16 lies a seventeen year old soldier, Private Albert Seel of 5/West Yorkshire, who died on 23 July 1915. Bradford soldier Private Joseph Ernest Wilkinson, 6/West Yorkshire, died of wounds on 17 November

1915 and lies in Row C Grave 15. It seems probable that he was seriously wounded by shell fire, for the War Diary records:

16 November. From 9.00 am to 3.30 pm enemy sent into our area about 100 Whiz Bangs and thirty heavies. Trenches in very bad condition. Weather frosty. 17 November, shelling at intervals by enemy with large calibre shells.

In Row C Grave 19 is Second Lieutenant Ernest Taylor, who died on 16 October 1915. The reader may recall 4/Duke of Wellingtons' defence of a sap and an abandoned communication trench in the Glimpse Cottage sector. Taylor was one of the twelve men killed or who died as a result of their wounds shortly afterwards.

Return to Vlamertingsestraat and, after the chateau, turn left; when you reach the junction with the N8 go straight ahead into Steenstraat. After fifty yards, turn right into Boezingsestraat; 500 yards along this road you will find, on your left, Bleuet Farm Cemetery (**10**), set back 150 yards from the road.

This was a major billeting area and a dressing station was established

Bleuet Farm Cemetery, a legacy of the dressing station once based here.

here at the beginning of the 1917 offensive. There are 437 United Kingdom, three South African, one Newfoundlander, one French and one German burials. In Plot 1 Row F Grave 8 lies 18389 Guardsman H J Cobb 1/Coldstream Guards, who died on 15 July 1917, aged seventeen. His headstone epitaph says, 'He was too young to fight and too young to die'.

Nearby in Grave 17 is a nineteen-year old lieutenant from 3 Company 3/Grenadier Guards, killed on 31 July 1917. His headstone states 'Killed at the Battle of Pilkem Ridge'.

In Plot 2 Row B are three men executed as a result of Field General Court Martial. Private T Hawkins, 7/Royal West Surrey, was a habitual offender who was executed for desertion on 22 November 1917, he is interred in Grave 12. Alongside him is Private Arthur H Westwood, 8/East Surrey, who had previously received ninety days field punishment for desertion. He also absented himself while his battalion was at Poelcapelle.

Guardsman H J Cobb, too young to fight and too young to die.

He was executed on 23 November 1917. Private Frederick Slade served as a stretcher-bearer with 2/6 London Regiment and had previously received ninety days field punishment for disobedience. During the Passchendaele offensive, on 26 October, Private Slade refused to parade before moving forward. He was arrested and tried. In defence he claimed to be traumatised by the horrors of war, but a medical officer declared the prisoner to be of sound mind. The death sentence was carried out on 14 December 1917. Private Slade is buried in Grave 33.

Return to your vehicle. Just ahead, on the right hand side, is a lane named Vroedenhofstraat, turn right and drive down the lane. In a bend in the road you pass Vroedenhof Farm and three-quarters of a mile from Boezingsestraat you reach a quiet junction. Turn left into Kapellestraat and head for a cemetery approximately 200 yards away. Facing the cemetery is Solferino Farm, named by the French troops who were holding the line here in 1915. Directly opposite, during October 1917, the

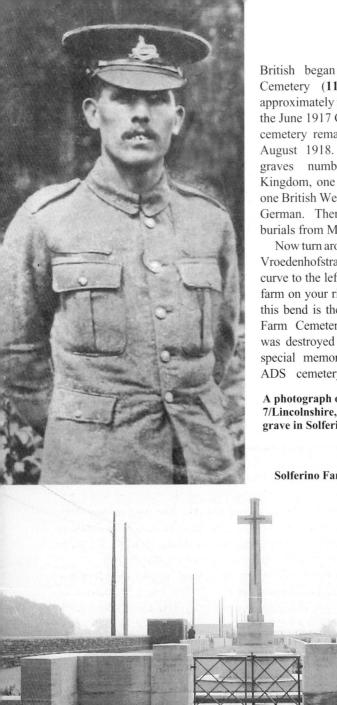

British began Solferino Farm Cemetery (**11**) which stands approximately two miles south of the June 1917 German lines. The cemetery remained in use until August 1918. The Great War graves number 293 United Kingdom, one Newfoundlander, one British West Indies and three German. There are also five burials from May 1940.

Now turn around and drive past Vroedenhofstraat. The road will curve to the left, and between the farm on your right hand side and this bend is the site of Malakoff Farm Cemetery. The cemetery was destroyed by shellfire, so a special memorial in Dulhallow ADS cemetery commemorates

A photograph of F D Rawson, 7/Lincolnshire, placed on his grave in Solferino Cemetery.

Solferino Farm Cemetery.

Loading a twelve-inch howitzer mounted on rolling stock near Brielen 1, August 1917.

the lost graves. Various battalion headquarters used the farm and the area was used by troops in support. The junction with the main road was a spot of evil repute, known as Dawson's Corner (**12**). The light railway from South Zwannof farm ran along the opposite side of the road in the direction of Elverdinghe. Artillery batteries were also sited here. Turn left, 350 yards from the junction is where the light railway once crossed the road.

Drive for about half a mile to Brielen, passing on your right four sets of buildings. Turn right 100 yards after the fourth building. The road splits into two carriageways, one is marked No Entry, take the left hand road. Go past the houses on your left and park at the top by the football pitch. To your right are two white pillars and a large gate, this is the entrance to Les Tres Tours Chateau (**13**), which is well concealed in private woodland. It is not possible, without consent, to visit this former headquarters, but at least puts it into context with all the other sites visited. Return to the N8 and turn left towards the N38 and Ypres, passing in the process through Brielen.

Gunner William Henry Towers, B Battery 245 Brigade RFA, spent a miserable period in the horse lines at Brielen:

It was a terrible place, they made it worse the officers. Where the horses stood, they did their business and all like that, it got sloppy and wet. Somebody had the bright idea of sending a party into Ypres, at night, with a wagon and dig the cobblestones up. Well this was taking an unnecessary risk, for they were shelling Ypres every night, and when we were throwing the cobblestones into the wagon, Gerry could hear the noise and started shelling. So we had to scarper, but that's what we had to do to make stone places for horses to stand on.

Follow the road to the junction of the N38; this concludes the tours.

Entering Boesinghe, 1921, the main street is lined with temporary housing for the returned inhabitants .

ORDER OF BATTLE

The 4th Division of 1915 comprised: *10 Brigade*– 1/Warwicks, 1/Royal Irish Fusiliers, 2/Seaforth Highlanders, 2/Dublin Fusiliers. *11 Brigade*– 1/Somersets, 1/Rifle Brigade, 1/East Lancashires, 1/Hampshire. *12 Brigade*– 1/Kings Own, 2/Essex, 2/Lancashire Fusiliers, and 2/Inniskillings, all regular battalions. Various corps and artillery completed each division.

The 49th (West Riding) Division of 1915 comprised: *146 Brigade*– 1/5th, 1/6th, 1/7th and 1/8th battalions of Prince of Wales's Own (West Yorkshire Regiment). *147 Brigade*– 1/4th, 1/5th, 1/6th, and 1/7th battalions of the Duke of Wellingtons (West Riding Regiment). *148 Brigade*– 1/4th and 1/5th Kings Own Yorkshire Light Infantry plus the 1/4th (Hallamshire) and 1/5th battalion of the York and Lancaster Regiment.

The 14th (Light) Division of early 1916 comprised: *41 Brigade*– 7th and 8th Kings Royal Rifle Corps and the 7th and 8th Rifle Brigade. *42 Brigade*– 5th Oxfordshire and Buckinghamshire Light Infantry (L.I), 5th Kings Shropshire LI, 9th Kings Royal Rifle Corps, and 9th Rifle Brigade. *43 Brigade*– 6th Prince Albert's Somerset LI, 6th Duke of Cornwall's LI, 6th Kings Own Yorkshire LI and 10th Durham LI. The 11th Kings Liverpool served as a pioneer battalion.

The 20th (Light) Division of 1916 included: *59 Brigade*– 10/Kings Royal Rifle Corps (KRRC), 11/KRRC, 10th and 11/Rifle Brigade. 59 MG Company and 59 TM Battery. *60 Brigade*– 6/Oxfordshire and Buckinghamshire LI, 6/ Kings Shropshire LI, 12/KRRC, 12 Rifle Brigade. 60 MG Company and 60 TM Battery. *61 Brigade*– 7/Somerset LI, 7/Duke Cornwall's LI, 7/Kings Own Yorkshire LI, 12/Kings Liverpool, 61 MG Company and 61 TM Battery. The 11/Durham LI were divisional pioneers.

The 38th (Welsh) Division infantry units in mid 1916 were: *113 Brigade*– 13th, 14th, 15th and 16th Royal Welsh Fusiliers. *114 Brigade*–10th, 13th and 14th and 15th Welsh Regiment. *115 Brigade*– 17th Royal Welsh Fusiliers, 10th and 11th South Wales Borderers. 16th Welsh Regiment. The 19th Welsh served as Pioneers. Artillery and various corps completed the force.

The Guards Division comprised: *1 Brigad*e- 2/Coldstream Guards, 3/Coldstream Guards, 1/Irish Guards, 2/Grenadier Guards. *2 Brigade*- 1/Coldstream Guards, 1/Scots Guards, 2/Irish Guards, 3/Grenadier Guards *3 Brigade*- 1/Welsh Guards, 1/Grenadier Guards, 2/Scots Guards, 4/Grenadier Guards.

SELECT BIBLIOGRAPHY AND
FURTHER READING

1/4 (Hallamshire) battalion. York and Lancaster Regiment, 1914-19 The. Captain D P Grant, MC, MA. Arden Press, Stamford Street, London, SE 1.

51st Division war sketches. (No 4 Bridge) Fred A Farrell. Edinburgh T C 86 Jack Ltd. 35 & 36 Paternoster Row. London. 1920.

A Deep Cry, Anne Powell. Palladour Books. Cartref, Aberporth, Cardigan, Dyfed. 1994.

Battlefields of the First World War, The. Peter Barton. Constable and Robinson Ltd, London. 2005.

Bravest of Hearts. The Liverpool Scottish in the Great War. Hal Giblin. Winordie Publications. Liverpool. 2002.

Douglas Haig's Despatches, Sir. J M Dent and Sons, London. 1919.

The German Army at Passchendaele, The. Jack Sheldon. Pen and Sword Books. 2007.

History of the First World War. B H Liddel Hart. Book Club Associates, London. 1979.

History of the 1/4 Duke of Wellington's (West Riding) Regiment 1914-1919. Captain P G Bales, CBE.

Halifax, Edward Mortimer Ltd, Regent Street, London. 1920.

Heart of a Dragon. Alistair Williams. Bridge Books. 2008.

History of the 38th (Welsh) Division, The. Lieutenant Colonel J E Munby, CMG, DSO. Hugh Rees, Ltd. 5 and 7, Regent Street, London. 1920.

History of the Sixth Battalion West Yorkshire Regiment, The. Captain E V Tempest DSO, MC. Percy Lund, Humphries & Co, Ltd. The County Press. Bradford. 1921.

Images of War, Jon Cooksey. Pen & Sword Ltd. 47 Church Street, Barnsley, South Yorkshire. 2008.

Irish Guards in the Great War, The. First Battalion. Rudyard Kipling. Spellmount Ltd. Stroud, Gloucestershire. 2008.

Irish Guards in the Great War, The. Second Battalion.

Kings Shropshire Light Infantry in the Great War 1914-1918, History of. Major W De B Wood. The Medici Society Limited, London. 1925.

Kitchener's Army. Ray Westlake. The Nutshell Publishing Co. Speldhurst, Kent. 1989.

Manual of Field Works (All Arms) 1925. HMSO. London.

Passchendaele. Nigel Steel and Peter Hart. Cassel Military Paperbacks. London. 2000.

Rats Alley, Peter Chasseaud. Spellmount Ltd. Stroud, Gloucestershire. 2006.

Recipients of the Distinguished Conduct Medal 1914 – 1920. R W Walker. Galata Coins Ltd, Wolverhampton. 1981.

Short History of the 6th Division, A. Major-General T O Marden CB, CMG. Hugh Rees Ltd, London, SW1. 1920.

Silent Cities, The. Sidney C Hurst. The Naval & Military Press. Old Bond Street, London. 1993.

Stand To. A diary of the trenches 1915-18. Captain F C Hitchcock M C. Hurst and Blackett Ltd, London. 1937.

Tunnellers. Captain W Grant Grieve and Bernard Newman. Herbert Jenkins Ltd. London. 1936.

War Walk, The. Nigel H Jones. Robert Hale Limited. Clerkenwell Green. London. 1983.

Welsh Outlook, The. Volume VI, 1919 p65-66 by Major W P Whelan DSO. The Welsh Outlook Press. Cardiff.

West Riding Territorials in the Great War, The. Laurie Magnus. Kegan Paul, Trench, Trubner & Co. Carter Lane, London. 1920.

Periodicals

Great War, I Was There, The. Part nine. The Amalgamated Press Ltd. Farringdon Street, London. 1938.

L'Illustration, Journal Universel. Number 3884. 13, Rue Saint-Georges, Paris. 11 August 1917.

Twenty Years After. (Various Parts) George Newnes Ltd. 8-11 Southampton Street, Strand, London.

Birkenhead News, The

Unpublished Sources

Two letters from 235276 Private Douglas Anderton. Courtesy of the Royal Welsh Fusiliers Archives.

The following war diaries consulted are availiable at the National Archives, Kew:

WO 95   335   173 Tunnelling Coy RE

	406	183 Tunnelling Coy RE
	1224	1/Welsh Guards
	1483	2/Seaforth highlanders
	1617	2/Durham LI
	1816	7/South Staffs
	1903	6/Somerset LI
	2121	12/Rifle Brigade
	2126	7/Duke Cornwalls LI
	2127	7/Somerset LI
	2275	1/York and Lancs
		2/York and Lancs
	2300	1/Lancashire Fusiliers
	2309	4/Worcestershire
	2555	13/Royal Welsh Fusiliers (RWF Archives)
		14/Royal Welsh Fusiliers (RWF Archives)
		15/Royal Welsh Fusiliers (RWF Archives)
		16/Royal Welsh Fusiliers (RWF Archives)
	2576	39 Division Signal Coy RE
	2794	6/West Yorks
	2795	1/7 West Yorks
		1/4 Duke of Wellingtons
		1/5 Duke of Wellingtons
		1/6 Duke of Wellingtons
	2805	1/4 York and Lancs (Hallamshires)
	2836	1/5 York and Lancs
	2882	7/Gordon Highlanders
WO 32	5876	49th Division Memorial debate

Trench Maps

WO 297	1727	Boesinghe corrected to 5 October 1915
		Boesinghe corrected to 10 January 1916
MF	1/8/9	RE sketch extracted from WO 95 335

"KAMERAD"

FINALE

INDEX